AVERAGE CHRISTIANS DON'T EXIST

ENCOURAGEMENT FOR BELIEVERS

By Kevin McSpadden

Garden Publishing Company, LLC

ISBN: 978-0-9833377-3-7
Copyright © 2012 by Kevin R. McSpadden
Book design, cover design, and formatting by Grant Hill
Photography by Jessica Dillbeck

Published in 2012 by The Garden Publishing Company.

Scripture taken from the New King James Version.
Copyright © 1982 by Thomas Nelson, Inc.
Used by permission. All rights reserved.

All rights reserved. No portion of this book may be reproduced,
stored in a retrieval system, or transmitted in any form by any
means, mechanical, electronic, photocopying, recording, or otherwise, without written permission from the publisher.

Printed in the U.S.A.

Garden Publishing Company, LLC
10403 US Highway 87 North
Sterling City, Texas 76951
http://gardenpublishingcompany.com

Dedication And Thanks

This book is dedicated to the love of my life, my wonderful wife Karen. My Beautiful One, you encourage me just by being around. I've learned so much about our Lord's heart from falling in love with you. I'm so glad I get to share my life with you and walk out these things as we learn and grow together. Thank you for believing in me with all your might, for listening to me talk animatedly about what the Lord is showing me even when I'm not making much sense, and for sharing this journey with me. You truly are a gift of the Lord to me greater than I could have asked or imagined.

Thanks to Brandy Helton, Lauren and Cliff Caldwell, Danetta and Dow Ferguson, Robin Reynolds, Brint and Robin Harmon, Grant and Amber Hill, and Nancy Hadley for your leadership and guidance. I wouldn't know my Jesus near as well as I do without all of you encouraging, correcting, and inspiring me. Thank you for pointing me to truth and showing me what it is to belong to a family in the Lord.

Thanks to Zeke Wayne for keeping my feet warm as I typed and for putting up with so many boring afternoons.

Foreword

It has been my honor and privilege to know Kevin McSpadden as a fellow believer in Jesus Christ and dear friend for quite some time. Watching Papa God transform this man over the years has been nothing short of supernatural. I have no doubt that God has raised him up to bring a revelation of the intimate love of the Father, true honor and our identity in the Kingdom of Heaven for such a time as this.

In *Average Christians Don't Exist*, Kevin McSpadden reveals facets of God's heart every believer needs to experience. Too many believers labor under inaccurate perceptions of what our God is really like. For too long being a Christian meant striving to love God more. How much love do we have to offer if we don't understand what it means to receive His love to begin with? 1 John 4:19 says, "We love Him because He first loved us."

Religion and tradition will often push us to work harder to be accepted. Our Father desires to open our eyes to His genuine affection toward us. Jesus does not merely tolerate us, He celebrates us. Holy Spirit invites and empowers us to run with Him. Let guilt, shame and performance die. When you and I genuinely experience the Love of God toward us we are made whole. It is a continual process of receiving. It is only then that we have true love to offer God and others.

Through this book you will be released to a deeper revelation of God's powerful love for you and all of His sons and daughters. By Kevin's personal stories, observations, and understanding, the truth will set you free. His words will inspire you to reflect upon your life with a different perspective. The world needs more "average" believers like Kevin McSpadden. May you be inspired to recognize your adventure with our King and fulfill the destiny planned just for you.

-Lauren Caldwell
    Author of *There's No Junior Holy Spirit: A Supernatural Training Manual for Youth*

Table of Contents

Author's Note

Thank you so much for allowing me the honor of sharing this with you. This book is an accumulation of some things God has given me over the years. It contains some of my favorite stories and revelations from my walk with my amazing Father. I'm passing them on to you for the sake of encouragement, edification, and exhortation.

I divided this book into chapters that are meant to be read in one sitting. Most of the chapters do not necessarily flow together, but the truths in all the chapters are closely related.

Scriptures for meditation accompany each chapter along with suggestions to make the ideas practical. I did not intend for this to be a teaching book, though you may very well learn some things along the way. Rather than present my ideas on what Scripture means, I decided to show how those truths have presented themselves in my life. My hope is that you'll be encouraged from my experiences and search these things out yourself with Holy Spirit as your guide.

You may read the chapters in order or skip around as you please. Whether you read straight through or use this book like a daily devotional, I strongly encourage you to take your time and allow Holy Spirit to talk to you about what you're reading. He will show you what you need to take from this book. He's a much better teacher than I am anyway.

1

In the Kingdom, There's No Such Thing As Average

I'll bet you a dollar that at some point in your life you've said something like this: "I'm just an average person. What good can I do?"

You've probably looked around at the people in your life and wished you could be more like them, with their perfect hair, perfect smiles, and perfect lifestyles. If only I could be more like Bob, you've thought to yourself, then I'd really be able to do something worthwhile.

So let me tell you something you really need to hear: you are awesome!

You may not believe me, and you may even think that's a really prideful thing for me to say to you. But I'm serious: whether you believe it or not, you are amazing! Your greatness, however, has very little to do with you and much more to do with Jesus.

Whose grace rescues sinners and changes lives? Whose goodness draws backsliders to repentance? Whose power heals the sick and raises the dead? Only the power of God called on through the name of Jesus by the guidance of Holy Spirit can perform these miracles. Yet, in His wisdom, God has planned an essential role for each believer to play in bringing His kingdom to the earth.

Ephesians 2:10 describes believers as the handiwork of God, noting that He has prepared good works in advance for believers to finish. His goodness sets up the circumstances, and His grace enables saints to perfect His plan. Furthermore, God's heart leaps with gladness when His people obey Him and complete the blueprint He prepared.

And there are no small plans in the heart of our eternal Father.

When God created the world, He designed each person as an indispensible part of His masterpiece. He carefully crafted every person in existence, and He never used a mold. Not one time did God get tired of forming each man and woman and say, "I think I'll pound out a couple just like this."

God created you the way you are, and He did it on purpose. Psalm 139 describes how your Father delicately knitted you together in your mother's womb. He knew what you would look like before you were born. He knew what would make you smile, what would make you cry, and what would ignite the flame of passion in your heart. Your personality, your destiny, and even your quirks were all His ideas.

And He did not have a single accident. God is precise. He spent an eternity before time dreaming of you, and the beautiful dreams of the Creator resulted in the person holding this book.

That's not to say you're perfect. If you're anything like me, you have no trouble pointing out all your faults. You're probably pretty good at describing why other people are so much more suitable to rock the world with the gospel of Jesus Christ. You may even feel you aren't quite ready for that yet.

When the Holy Spirit inspired Paul to urge His people to work out their salvation, He knew Christians would wrestle with their shortcomings. Though our complete salvation is already an accomplished fact in the spirit as soon as we make Jesus our Lord, we believers must allow Him to accomplish it as a fact in our souls and bodies. Each has attained a different degree of freedom and revelation, but none has fully arrived.

I don't personally know a single person whom God has

yanked up into the heavens because they had completed all He had planned for them and He was ready to bring them home. The whole Bible only records three such people: Enoch, Elijah, and Jesus.

Still, the Holy Spirit has planted deep in your heart spectacular dreams and beautiful desires to accomplish great works for the One you love. And it is because of that beautiful lover of your soul that you can be, will be, and currently are an extraordinary person.

Yet, tons of Christians just like you and me frown on ourselves and make the declaration that we're just "average." Nobody knows our name, and most of us feel we've not yet done anything that has shaken the earth. Some days we're struggling just to make it though. Therefore, according to this mindset, we're not worthy to accomplish great things for Jesus. We're not spiritual enough, or we just don't have the knowledge or training we need.

Many Christians have adopted the viewpoint that only the pastors, worship leaders, or evangelists can truly be powerful in faith. After all, that's what we pay them to do, so it makes sense that they should be the ones carrying the kingdom of heaven to the world. Compared to them, what could an "average" Christian possibly have to offer?

The belief that so-called "average" Christians are powerless has crept into our consciousness through poor understanding of who we really are, lack of revelation of God's amazing love, and unbelief in the full power of our Lord Jesus. Either we have underestimated God's unlimited power, or we have not believed that He really does unleash it through our lives.

Someone who truly believes he is just average does not set out on grand journeys with the Creator. He may applaud the effort of the brave elite, but he cowers in the shadows of what he perceives to be his own failures and shortcomings. Someone convinced of his own plainness has enormous difficulty seeing himself as worthy of love, especially the immense magnitude of love God has for him.

The mentality that most Christians are simply average is a leech draining believers of their strength and leaving them feeling too weak to pursue the magnificent destiny God designed for every last one of them.

That mentality needs to die a violent death, and it needs to happen right now. Jesus chose us as His bride. He elected us into His kingdom of priests. He happily calls us brothers and friends. Apparently Jesus sees something worthwhile and special in each of us. The time has come to see through His eyes and live from His heart.

Friend, what would you say if I suggested to you that you have super powers? What if you had the power to save any sick person wasting away on a death bed? What if you could invest in something that would produce at least a 30-fold return? What if your love could transform a prostitute into a princess? What if you could dash daringly into a battle wielding a sword whose power struck terror into the hearts of your enemies?

Would you still think of yourself as average?

These powers are not suggestions or daydreams, but promises issued to all of us by Jesus Himself. He commanded that we heal the sick, cleanse the lepers, raise the dead, and freely give whatever we freely received from Him. He taught that what we sow, we reap pressed down, shaken together, and running over. He sent us to preach the gospel to every nation, allowing the power of the love of Christ to transform even the worst scumbag alive into an heir of the kingdom, a prince of heaven.

That's reality. And that kind of power is available to every person who truly belongs to Jesus Christ. It comes from knowing God intimately, hearing His voice, and loving Him enough to trust Him and do what He says.

This walk we're on is all about the love of an incredible God. We must receive that love, bathe in it like fragrant oil, and leak that perfume all over the world. Effort and intellectual resolve are useless. Only love can sustain and direct us.

Some people reading this right now are weary from the journey. They've worked hard and found themselves left dry as a prune, lacking the joy that once spurred them on. Others think of God as a distant figure, sitting off somewhere in space and frowning at how average we are and how little we do correctly. Some are exasperated because they desperately want to do great things for Jesus, but they just don't think it's possible. Then there's the category I hope you're in, the ones on fire for Jesus, living in His love, and just looking for a little fuel for the flame.

Whatever your circumstance, I can tell you with absolute certainty that the answer to your dilemma and the solution to your problem is the unconditional love of God the Father. It is the dynamite power of Holy Spirit. It is the promise of Jesus Christ. It all comes down to love.

My purpose in writing this book is to urge my fellow believers on toward the love of God. Just to establish that I'm worthy to write this, let me take a moment to list all my qualifications.

There, I'm glad that's over.

I'm not a pastor, not a founder of a movement, and definitely not someone you'd pay money to see at a conference (not yet, anyway). I am just a guy who loves Jesus and who has learned a thing or two about Him along the way.

My story, which you'll get to know more of later, is probably a lot like yours. I was in a deep, dark hole, wallowing in misery, but Jesus rescued me and transformed my life. He changed how I think, altered how I act, and even empowered me to love people, including myself.

Even better than that, He talks to me, and He uses language I can understand. He wants me to know Him, just like He wants you to know Him. This book is a collection of memories, stories, pictures, and revelations I've received over the years that have each helped me understand a part of what God is like. Every one of them has inspired me, challenged me, or convicted me. But every one of them has revealed more and more of the earth-shaking love my God has for me.

And one part of that revelation is that in God's eyes there

is no such thing as an average Christian.

Each of us truly is a unique individual created to occupy a place in the kingdom of heaven that only we can fill. No one else can do it. God designed things so that we would all depend on each other because we have no other choice! And He made it so that we would have to depend completely on Him. God is counting on every single one of us. No exceptions. He's calling us to believe in Him above all else, and He's opening eyes to see the glory He placed in every one of His children.

I hope that by the time you finish reading this book, you realize more of just how special you truly are. I hope you are challenged, convicted, and broken. I hope you are refreshed and that your passion leaps up within you like an oil well gushing up from the deep. I hope you discover, or perhaps re-discover, just how accessible our God is and just how much He desires great things for you.

I hope the dreams of your heart that you've allowed to wilt or die will come springing back to a joyfully resurrected vitality. I hope you discover more of who you truly are in Jesus and what a spectacular life it is to serve the Living God, not wishing and hoping for good, but living out the dreams He planted within you.

Most of all, I pray you'll fall more in love with Jesus, or that you fall in love with Him for the first time. That, after all, is the reason we're alive.

Remember, even Elijah was "just" a man. If he could pray and open or shut the heavens, what incredible plan might God have for you? Jesus promised that those who believe in Him will do greater exploits even than He did. What miracles, signs, and wonders did our beautiful Lord design to take place beneath your hands? God says we're His kids. What astonishing treasure trove will He reach into just to give you a gift, just because He likes you?

Your journey awaits you, and excitement and joy are beckoning. Holy Spirit is nudging. Jesus is calling. God the Father is looking on in delighted anticipation. It's time.

Bon voyage!

Scriptures for meditation:

Psalm 139
Jeremiah 29:11
Hebrews 11:6
Ephesians 1:15-23

Make it real:

• Ask Holy Spirit to show you any areas where you have underestimated or not trusted in God's power. Repent for unbelief and doubt and ask Him to remove those things from you and replace them with faith.

• Ask Holy Spirit to open your eyes so you can see yourself as He sees you.

• Ask Holy Spirit to show you Jesus as He truly is and to reveal Jesus' love to you.

• Ask for humility, which will protect you from being puffed up, and for the fear of the Lord, which will help you see yourself as He does.

• Ask God for a fresh filling with Holy Spirit and a new hunger for the presence of the Lord.

Part One: Treasure In An Earthen Vessel

God once showed me an immense treasury in heaven, brimming with jewels, gold coins, and every article of value I could have imagined. It sparkled brilliantly, drawing my eyes from place to place and stealing my breath.

Then Father poked me and said, "Kevin, this is not treasure. This is building material." Slightly confused, I felt God direct my attention behind me, where a host of people gathered, watching. God told me, "This is treasure."

Your life is a treasure. Your very existence is a precious gift from God Himself, filled with experiences and people who have made it rich. While not all of your memories may be pleasant, sitting down with Father God and looking at the pictures shows just how close He has been in all those times.

These are some of my stories, my pictures in Father's album. He's taught me that some of His deepest pleasure comes from the everyday. Sometimes God hides the most amazing revelation in the simplest places.

2

The Legend of Kramitall Inn

The family station wagon pounded down a dusty country road just south of Colorado City, Texas. I leaned as far forward as I could, looking over my dad's shoulders to try to get a glimpse of the most mystical place on earth according to my seven-year-old mind.

Up ahead a familiar sign swayed from an iron bumper gate. "McSpadden's Kramitall Inn," it bragged. The Kramitall Inn, seated on the shores of Champion Creek Reservoir, was the majestic home of a famous and powerful warrior, who also happened to be seven years old.

Kramitall Inn was the name my grandpa had given the little two-room cabin he leased so the family would have a getaway spot. "If you want to get your stuff in there, you have to cram it all in," he laughed. Though most people would find it unimpressive, this little hideaway provided the dreamscape for all the adventure a seven-year-old could hope for.

I stepped from the station wagon and into the boundless world of my imagination, taking note of the state of affairs after my absence. A salt cedar forest loomed up to swallow the tiny cabin. A hundred steps from the house stood the lakeshore, where I heard the taunting call of monster catfish just begging to be caught. Imps and dragons prepared for the battle they knew I would wage against them the next day. Somewhere in the darker regions of my mind, an invincible enemy raised a war cry and defied me to come and fight.

By this time, I was no longer Kevin, the insecure little boy. I was the Gladiator. No fish and no imaginary foe stood a chance.

Every trip to the Kramitall Inn took me on different adventures. Every time was special. Even now, I can feel the thrill of excitement rise as I think about the fun I always had there. It was my private place where I could just be who I really was without fear of judgment or ridicule. To a seven-year-old, such places are invaluable.

On a rickety wooden dock my grandpa had built, I learned the joys of fishing. A normal day at the lake found me manning my post on the dock before the sun showed its sleepy face. I would fish until it got too hot, then I would swim until my arms were full of lead. Or I might sneak off for one of my secret adventures. Later in the evening, after a hearty chili dog dinner, I would head back down to the water and fish until my eyes refused to stay open.

After a long day of fishing or other miscellaneous adventures, my family would all retire to the "living room" of the Kramitall Inn. My brother and I shared an air mattress on the floor, while Mom and Dad used a queen-sized bed that rested in one corner of the room. When Grandma and Grandpa were there, they got the bed and my folks pulled out another air mattress.

Despite being stuffed into our sleeping arrangement like matches in a box, I still found entertainment during nights at Kramitall Inn. Something about staying up and listening to a chili dog-inspired orchestra fascinates a young boy. Maybe the methane messed with my head, but I could stay awake for hours giggling and guessing in the dark. I could even tell my family's farts apart. I maintain that you have not lived until you have heard your grandfather rattle the bed frame with an atomic blast. One time, I could have sworn he actually rose off the bed. It was awesome.

The best thing about Kramitall Inn, other than the great fishing, was that it gave me a place to be out of my parents' sight. I learned an awful lot from that time alone. The lessons, which I stick to even now, included some of the following: Never throw a stick at a wasp's nest. Always make sure there are no big rocks in the water before you dive in. Never, ever let your mom catch you swimming naked. If your mom does catch you swimming naked, learn Spanish and head for Guatemala.

Kramitall Inn even had some serious lessons to offer. After all, it brought out the fighter in my heart. Often, during my unsupervised time, my young imagination would run rampant, and I turned into the unbeatable warrior, the Gladiator.

Armed with a "bright sword," usually a thick stick I would rigorously test for strength, I waded into the dead salt cedars, vanquishing dragons, evil wizards, or entire armies of really bad dudes. In my time, I have laid waste to millions of skinny dead trees, which had temporarily transformed into some villain or another. The main bad guy, though, was a giant dead tree with sprawling limbs that I nicknamed "the Spider."

The Spider, menacing and deadly, often foiled my attempts at heroism. The Spider lived in the dark recesses of my mind, sharing its house with my fears and insecurities. It mocked with the voices of my schoolmates. It knew all my secrets, all my shame. It was so strong that no stick could break its powerful legs, and no amount of force could scathe it. Time after time, I fought it. Time after time, I retreated, stick broken, arms and legs bleeding from scratches, disappointed that I had failed yet again. But I never gave up.

Finally, I hatched a brilliant plan. My grandmother possessed a magically enhanced staff which I believed would overpower the Spider's armor. It was a mop with a metal handle. I swiped the metal staff, removed the mop (which I saw as useless anyway), and went back to do battle.

This time, I triumphed. The Spider got in one blow when I tripped over a rock and scraped my arm, but I returned with a fury that has never been rivaled in the history of imaginary warfare. I smashed and beat at the vicious beast until at last one of its legs gave way to the magical staff. Victory!

Never mind that the mop handle was completely mangled. Never mind that when my grandmother found out later what I did to her mop, she mangled my behind. I had broken The Spider's leg. Nothing else mattered.

Once I understood that I could beat it, the Spider never seemed quite so scary. In my battles after that day, I would often look at it and wonder how it had ever defeated me, the Gladiator. It seemed as if I had passed a test. I had become something altogether different and much stronger than I was before. I like to imagine that I am that thing now.

Today, my life is still filled with Spiders, challenges that loom up and make me feel so small and weak. I still fight battles that leave me bleeding and disappointed, though I no longer use swords that I can actually swing.

Every one of us faces battles that make us feel incredibly small and insignificant. The problems loom over us threateningly, and temptation whispers in our ears that we should just back down and avoid the struggle.

Yet, in every one of our hearts live mighty warriors, aching for the chance to rise up and engage the enemy valiantly. After all, we are made in the image of Father God, whose many names include Victorious Warrior and Mighty Awesome One. That's why even in the darkest of our struggles that part of us says, "Get up and fight! You can win!"

That part of us is telling us the truth.

Sometimes, it just takes one more trip to the frontlines. Sometimes, it is one more swing of your sword, one more prayer, one more act of love that defeats the enemy. One more fight may yet win the battle. And afterward, looking at that foe who seemed so unbeatable for so long, we will realize it's not so big and bad after all. Greater is He who is in us than those who oppose us.

When the Spiders rise up against the saints of God, throwing venomous darts of discouragement and doubt, we must allow that warrior God planted in each of us to rise up, lift up the sword, bellow a war cry, and enter the battle. We may not win this time, but next time we just may. Sooner or later, the current foe will be vanquished, and the saints will prevail.

If you were to visit the Kramitall Inn now, all you'd find is a dry lake bed and a crumbling cabin that has been swallowed by time and weeds. You probably wouldn't believe that I once pulled upward of a hundred fish out of that place in one weekend. You wouldn't see the bad guys that needed killing, and you probably wouldn't understand why remembering that place is so important to a grown man.

To me, though, nothing could be more important. Kramitall Inn helped me discover an important part of who I am.

Beloved, all of us must remember that the numbers of the mighty men and women of valor didn't end with the Bible. The world needs warriors today, probably more than ever. The warriors live inside the people of God. It's time to let them out.

Scriptures for meditation:

Psalm 24:7-10
2 Chronicles 20:1-30
Revelation 19:11-16
Jeremiah 20:11-12
Zephaniah 3:17

Make it real:

God truly is an almighty, undefeated warrior, and He resides in you. The battles you're fighting do not belong to you, but to Him. You act as His representative, bringing His will to earth as you overcome by His might. Ask Holy Spirit to show you the battles you're fighting in which you aren't seeing God's victory. Surrender those battles to Him in Jesus' name. Wait for God to show you how and when to fight. Thank God in advance for the victories He will win on your behalf.

3

Dying for Love

"I can't believe I'm actually going to do this."

Those words echoed around the interior of my Saturn Ion, freshly gassed up and ready for the impending trip to a city I never had even the slightest desire to visit. The echo seemed to say to me, "I can't either."

I checked all my stuff one last time. If I happened to forget anything, there was no chance of coming back to get it. One does not simply return from a twelve hundred mile trip for the toothbrush he didn't manage to get into his bag. My two duffel bags, one red, one black, rested in the backseat underneath my crisp toiletry bag, all practically brimming with my provisions for the trip. I had bags of snacks in the front seat, green wasabi-coated peas guaranteed to set my nostrils on fire if I ate too many at once. A blue Dasani water bottle graced my cup holder, glistening in the morning light. The trunk was completely filled with razors, toothbrushes, and lotion bottles, gifts I'd be leaving at my destination, the Dream Center.

"Okay," I told myself. "Guess this is it. Let's go."

With those words, I pulled out of my driveway and steered my car west toward the city of angels, which awaited me at the end of the longest trip I'd ever made by myself. Though I did suspect I was about to undergo a change, I never could have imagined the depth of transformation that would soon take place in my life.

Many of us look back at decisions we have made and wonder, what exactly was it that got us to do that? Maybe inspiration had been stalking us like a tiger in the brush, waiting for the precise moment to spring out and trap us into greatness. Maybe we held desires within us that our conscious mind, with all its "what-ifs" and "cannots," had yet to discover. Maybe those desires met up with inspiration at just the right time and combined to transform the what-ifs into why-nots.

The decision to make the trip to Los Angeles invaded my consciousness one lazy afternoon while watching television. I was purposefully wasting a day in front of the boob tube, letting the couch slowly devour me like a python and washing myself in the neon glow from the screen.

I had turned the channel to the Trinity Broadcasting Network, perhaps looking for some substance to break the monotony of pure brain candy upon which I had been feasting. That's when a Spirit-filled man popped onto the screen and seized me by the heart.

His name was Matthew Barnett. Young and enthusiastic, his passion practically glowed through the television frame. He was a guest on a prominent faith-based show, discussing his lifelong passion: the Dream Center.

Pastor Barnett started the Dream Center at the age of twenty with one goal in mind: to take the love of Christ to the darkest corners of one of America's toughest cities. Almost two decades later, the Dream Center has grown to a massive sanctuary of faith in a city of bustle and decay, a hulking arena of love nestled into the very heart of fear.

The Dream Center, so named because its mission was to restore the dreams of the people it ministers to by showing them the true love of Christ, was not a place for the weak at heart. The people who served there willingly went into the roughest neighborhoods, often with food for the hungry, many times with games and fun for the kids living in those places, but always with love for whoever needed it. Skid Row, the red light district, and South Central may be places a normal pastor would avoid, but the Dream Center deliberately targeted these places. The people there needed the most love. And love, as Pastor Barnett said, was the most important aspect of the whole Dream Center.

"Everything we do is designed to build relationships," he said. "We want people to know that we care about them, regardless of who they are or what they look like."

As I sat on my couch, aroused from my stupor by Pastor Barnett and his life mission, the thought slammed into my mind like a Mack truck into a brick wall: I'm going there. Little did I know that I was actually prophesying to myself.

I think what convinced me to go to Los Angeles was the straightforward challenge Barnett offered to his viewers: if you really believe your God is bigger than the problems of the world, then your life should be proof. Plain and simple.

I loved Jesus with all my heart, but when had I ever put my life on the line for His sake? I went to church and believed in helping people when I could, but when had I ever made a serious sacrifice on His behalf? I did believe He could do anything, but when had my life given Him the opportunity for miracles?

In my heart I heard Jesus saying, "He who loves his life will lose it, but he who loses his life for My sake shall keep it." It was decided: I had to leave behind everyone and everything I loved and go where I had always been terrified to go.

But Los Angeles? Didn't every person there have a gun and know how to use it?

The movies and television always made LA seem like the kind of place where you were lucky if you lived to be thirty years old. Between the crazies and the gangs and the fast-lane lifestyle, I was fairly certain I would not survive two days in that city. Yet, I could not ignore it. I tried to forget what I had said that day on the couch, but the thought simply would not go away.

Almost three years after I saw Pastor Barnett on TV, I finally worked up the courage to go. I made the trip across the country to Los Angeles, California. It felt like death for me, but it was also a journey of love. It was like my heart was saying, "See Lord, I love you enough to do this for you." At the same time, my mind was screaming the exact opposite.

My first impression of Los Angeles, with its towering skyscrapers and swarms of people everywhere, was that it would eat me alive. I saw it through the eyes of fear, and fear can magnify any gnat of a problem so that it looks like a dragon.

I was afraid that I would not be up to the task. I was afraid that the people there would simply chew me up, spit me out, and rob me just for good measure. I was afraid that I would fail where so many others had succeeded. Yet, even in the face of these fears, I still reported for duty as a volunteer at the Dream Center.

One of the first things I learned helping at the Dream Center was that it was practically impossible to differentiate between the "good" and the "bad" on the basis of looks. I cannot tell how many times I was completely intimidated by someone only to find out they were on full time staff as a ministry leader or something similar.

I also learned that sometimes there was a darker reason why someone may have gone to such effort to appear trustworthy. I felt like the world had gone backwards. The former convict with the tattoos all over his body couldn't stop talking about how much he loved Jesus, while the slick dude in the business suit lurked outside a store trying to pick pockets.

I quickly found that I needed to get the plank out of my earthly eyes and start looking at people with the eyes of Jesus. I would never be able to tell who was who without Holy Spirit discernment. The many encounters with the diverse people there challenged my faulty stereotypes and continually showed me the depth of my wrong thinking.

Outing after outing with the staff of the Dream Center proved that most people, even in the streets of Los Angeles, respond positively when treated with respect. The homeless, the tough, and the upper class all seemed pleasantly surprised when volunteers showed them a friendly face and genuine concern for their well-being.

Along with that, I found that the more I tried to care for others, the less I worried about what would happen to me. Though fear never stopped nagging me, it reverted to its miniscule form, and I could simply swat it whenever it came around.

Suddenly I found myself walking up to complete strangers asking if I could pray for them or inviting them to the children's service we were organizing that afternoon. I shifted fearlessly into broken Spanish so I could talk to the cold-eyed teenagers sitting in the park with nowhere better to go. I didn't care that I probably sounded like an idiot to them. All I could think about was trying to help them however I could.

Even on Skid Row, when a scraggly-bearded man with two metal objects walked up to me, brandished his weapons, and glared into my face, I was surprisingly calm. I did take note that I could possibly get hurt very quickly, but somehow I was able to look into his eyes and listen to what he said, most of which made absolutely no sense. The idea of running never came into my mind.

By the end of my short time at the Dream Center, I had become a new person. I was not free from attacks of fear, but I was definitely no longer dominated by it. Even things that should scare me didn't seem so terrible in the light of God's love.

In that respect my trip to Los Angeles really was a death. The Kevin McSpadden who used to be intimidated walking into Wal-Mart in San Angelo, Texas, after dark had passed away.

Additionally, being at the Dream Center taught me that fear is the opposite not of courage, but of love. Someone who is in love does not care about the cost of his actions. That person is simply concerned with giving away the treasure he carries in his heart. Love disarms enemies, protects hearts, and grows courage. Where there are great lovers, there will always be courageous fighters.

That, I have learned, is why a twenty-year-old could move to Los Angeles with around forty of his friends and create one of the nation's largest and most effective ministry centers. He was in love with his God. Therefore, Matthew Barnett and the things the stood for were unstoppable.

I discovered that I, too, carry within myself a treasure that makes me an overcomer. The love I have for my friends, my family, and my God is a flame that consumes the nagging of fear. Fear destroys itself, but love only grows stronger as it is expressed. I earnestly hope I continue to find myself thinking, "I can't believe I'm about to do this." Each time I'm in that circumstance, I'm sure that who I am will soon die. But I also know that love will resurrect me again, stronger, surer, and even less afraid.

Scriptures for meditation:

1 John 4:17-21
Psalm 23
Luke 6:37-42
Mark 9:34-38
Exodus 3

Make it real:

•   If you really believe in the greatness of God, your life should be proof. Pray and ask God to bind up and remove any condemnation you feel from that statement.

•   Ask Holy Spirit to show you all the ways your life glorifies Jesus, and don't reject anything as "too little." Honor Him again for all He shows you.

•   The enemy often uses fear to attack you in areas where you are powerfully anointed by the Lord. Ask Holy Spirit to reveal what you fear, and repent for participating with that fear. Ask for new eyes of love.

•   Pray Philippians 1:9-11 over yourself and receive what you pray.

4

Swing Away

In my hometown, the first Little League game of the year had finally arrived. My team, ahead for our final at-bat, clung to a small lead with two outs. The runners on first and second base depended on me to drive them in and score runs that would keep us ahead. The hard-throwing lefty on the mound was tiring, but still slinging some nasty pitches. I stepped into the box and fixed him with my best stare. People in these kinds of situations talk about butterflies in their stomachs. I had grizzly bears doing the cha-cha in mine. This at-bat would be a defining moment in my final season as a Little Leaguer.

Despite the pressure, there was nowhere else I'd rather be. When I was in Middle School, the baseball diamond was my place to shine. The sound of crickets mixed with fuzzy loudspeakers. The smell of cigarette smoke wafted like championship dreams through the outfield, and the crunch of the base path beneath my cleats told me this was my time. And it was time I desperately needed.

Middle School knocked me flat on my rear like a chin-high fastball. Suddenly, my two major school talents (answering every single stinking question every single stinking teacher asked, and the ability to fart at will) brought on resentment instead of unbridled adoration from my peers. As if that wasn't enough, I had gained quite a bit of weight.

Nobody in Middle School likes the fat, smelly teacher's pet.

To make things worse, girls started getting totally weird, and perfectly reasonable guys started doing crazy things like putting on deodorant and – combing their hair?   The world stopped making sense in Middle School.

I'm no expert in these matters, but I would guess many people begin to experience rejection around Middle School age. The pressure to fit in squeezes the uniqueness out of us, while the search for who we are suddenly becomes a cloudy maze. To this day, I still find myself seeking healing for wounds from my days in Middle School.

Even then, however, at least baseball was still baseball. Pretty boys and fat guys got along on the diamond. Girls still had enough sense to cheer from the stands, and some even played. When adrenaline and the unyielding desire to win took over, cliques and twelve-year-old pettiness were crushed like grass under cleats. And I was good at baseball.

When I was eleven, I pitched the final game of the season against the undefeated Cardinals. Our chances at winning the pennant had already died, but my Dodgers could still take out the only unbeaten team left in the league. Five innings into the game, my team trailed by one run and the time limit was coming up quick. The Cardinals were batting, and all they needed were a couple of hits to stall and run out the time. I pitched with all I had, striking out the side in time to earn my team another at-bat.

We had the top of our lineup coming to the plate in the last inning. The Cardinals switched to a fresh pitcher, trying to keep us from scoring the two runs we would need to win the game. The new pitcher was too nervous, though, and walked the first two batters before striking the third one out in three pitches. My turn.

Somehow, I wasn't nervous that time. That was the chance I had waited for all year. I bounced the first pitch he threw off the fence and drove in what would turn out to be the winning run. After that game, I strode victoriously off the field – the envy of the league. I ended the season and the school year as a Little League hero.

Unfortunately, the following school year wiped my triumph from the minds of my peers. My grades were still excellent, but neither the teachers nor my classmates appreciated my immaturity. I became less and less popular. I clung to any hint of friendship like a grass burr to knee-high socks, but time after time found myself being used.

Only now do I fully realize how urgently I needed baseball season to arrive. I craved the opportunity to do something right, to stand out in a good way. When the first game did arrive, I found myself facing that hard-throwing lefty, once again in a position to save the day.

As he wound up, I forced myself to stay calm. Don't blow it. Wait for a good one. I watched a couple pitches go by, but I finally did see one I liked, a chest-high fastball, right in my wheelhouse. I parked that sucker over the center field fence and trotted around the bases like I knew that was exactly what would happen.

The game turned out not to be a close one, but the game really wasn't the most important thing for me that night. I had come through for my team again, and it felt terrific. I went on to help my team win the league, an exciting end to my career as a Little Leaguer.

When I reflect on the self-esteem I took from baseball, I can see how all of my peers were exactly like me in one respect. All of them needed a chance to do something special.

Competition, rejection, and envy work together to convince people they have nothing special to offer the world or the Lord. If you're not the best, you don't matter. If people don't like you, you can't live out your dreams. And if someone else can do it better than you, why should you bother?

Yet, the kingdom of heaven offers every believer exactly what baseball offered me: a place to shine. God does not reject anyone because someone else can perform better. God doesn't require that we be the best of everyone, He only asks that we be the best we can be.

And God sets us up to win! Not only has He specially created works for us in advance (Ephesians 2:10), He has also given us the Holy Spirit to empower us to carry out the works. That's like batting in the last inning with the winning run on base and the pitcher lofting a lolly-pop for you to crank into the outfield bleachers.

It's a game Father loves to play because His kids always win. He has set up circumstances, meetings, and opportunities for saints to win the game. He has specially crafted each individual with the exact combination of personality and ability to succeed, and He loves it when we come through for Him. Just like my chances to shine as a pre-teen came on the baseball diamond, every believer has a chance to shine with Jesus. Best of all, there are no strikeouts with Him. He gives us unlimited swings and at-bats, and He doesn't relent until we hit the homerun.

The trick is to keep swinging.

When things don't look the way we think they should, it becomes easy to leave the bat on our shoulders. Sometimes the pitches look unhittable, or the game feels un-winnable, but there's no excuse not to swing.

Remember that God prepared the works in advance, and He created each of us specifically to finish those works. The only way we fail is not to act. The only strikeouts happen when we don't swing.

All of us have a champion living inside our hearts, waiting for the right opportunity to leap out and bring heaven to its feet with applause. Flaws, limitations, and even the cruel expectations of failure from our peers cannot hold that champion down when the time comes. Under the right conditions, even a cloud of dust can become a star. Sometimes, a homerun is just a confident swing away.

Scriptures for meditation:

Ephesians 2:10
1 John 1:7-9
Jeremiah 32:38-41
Matthew 19:26
Philippians 4:8-13

Make it real:

• Ask Holy Spirit to reveal any wounds from your past that have continued to affect you. As he brings them up, forgive the people responsible, and if necessary, forgive yourself. Remember forgiveness is not an emotion, it is a choice.
• Re-read at least one of your favorite Bible stories. Record in your journal all the ways you see that God set His people up to succeed. Ask Him to do the same thing for you.
• Think of something at which you excel. Praise God for your giftings in that area. Ask Him to show you a way to use those giftings deliberately for His glory.

5

Audacity

"I'll go anywhere and pray for anybody because I ain't scared o' nothin'!"

The man saying those words was not boasting; he was merely stating a fact. No bravado or swagger accompanied his remark, just a calm yet determined expression that showed he meant what he said. Imagine someone telling you that it's really cold in Antarctica as if they've spent time there and they're stating something obviously true. That's how David Spray looked as he proclaimed what I take to be his life mission: taking the good news of Jesus, especially His healing and salvation, to the sick, hurting, and dying.

As far as David is concerned, the worse the situation and the more desperate the need, the greater chance for the light of Christ to shine.

When I first met David Spray and his wife Barbara, I felt like I had re-discovered a long-lost uncle and aunt. His modest, unassuming manner and his quick and quirky sense of humor put me instantly at ease. It did not take long, however, for me to recognize a hard-earned wisdom behind the playful glint in his eyes. Barb's easy smile and gentle nature form the perfect complement. They just fit together.

You could probably walk right by the Sprays in Wal-Mart and never know just how close you came to being miraculously touched. That is, you could until they started speaking to you and you found yourself washed in a river of truth, love, and mercy. That tends to happen when David or Barb open their mouths.

David wasn't kidding, either, when he said he'd go anywhere and tell anybody about Jesus. So far, I've heard about a man who could barely leave his trailer because of health, an HIV positive homeless man diving in a dumpster, a recently released convict, and several dozen other similar people who have heard the gospel and been touched by the Lord because David and Barb took the time to reach out to them. Where most people would back away in fear or disgust, David strolls up and starts conversations, which usually end in hugs.

And it's not like he knows karate or something. He's not very big, either, standing around 5'8" and probably not much over 160 pounds. He is just not scared. He closely resembles the Israelite king who also bears his name: he knows who his God is, and he's more confident in Him than he is scared of whoever he talks to. So no matter where he is, what's happening, or who is there, David preaches Jesus.

He is also blessed to have the perfect companion for his adventures. Barb tends to be quieter than David, but she lives from a tender heart. Perfect strangers willingly receive her hugs. A reassuring glance from Barb's eyes and a touch from her gentle hands releases courage and revitalization. She's also a powerful prophetic intercessor who's simply not afraid to follow where Jesus leads.

Quite frankly, David and Barbara Spray are two of the most audacious people I know.

I mean that in the best possible way, and I wouldn't say it without their understanding of what I mean. Recently, in one of our church (read "family") gatherings at the Garden Apostolic Training Center, which we attend together, Holy Spirit pointed them out to me and whispered that word into my ear. I had to agree because it fits them so perfectly.

Would you walk into the territory of your worst enemy and talk to his people about his biggest rival? Would you step up to a disease-infested woman and tell her she had no right to be sick? Would you demand that a stump of an arm grow back to its original form and then wait and watch for it to happen? If someone told you about a man with several infirmities and handicaps who was decidedly against receiving prayer, would your first words be, "We're going to go pray for him, and he's going to be healed"?

That kind of audacity is the exact kind that Jesus had. The Lord had no problem telling people the kingdom of heaven was at hand. It didn't faze Him to proclaim the fulfillment of Scripture in a crowd of people who didn't believe in Him, nor did it bother Him to defeat legions of demons in a man no one else would even approach. Jesus was pretty audacious, or so it seemed to the people of the time, because He didn't let traditions or situations stop Him from doing His Father's work.

He was audacious enough to love even when love wasn't welcome.

How sad is it that we live in a world where doing good seems offensive? When Dave tells cancer patients Jesus is about to heal them, they look at him like he just grew another head. The doctors say it will take weeks and months of chemotherapy and probably surgery to get the cancer out, but David suggests he can heal it right there. What arrogance! Even other believers frown at such a proclamation.

"What if he prays and nothing happens?" they fret. "What if that causes the person to doubt God? You just shouldn't get people's hopes up like that. And besides, who is he to contradict the wisdom of the medical industry?"

He's a son of the Most High God, that's who.

Someone in authority has no problem going into a situation and demanding that things change. Bosses do it. Teachers do it. Why not saints? If we really are children of God, we're a part of the Royal Family of heaven, so why does it seem so rude for us to demand that things line up with the will of God? It shouldn't appear strange or uncouth because that's exactly what God wants. In Matthew 6:10, Jesus taught His followers to pray that very thing. He loves it when His kids march into the devil's territory and tear it down. And He loves it even more when His people take their eyes off the darkness and focus on Him.

Something happens when we stop looking at the circumstances, stop listening to the critics and the doubtful, and start seeing through the eyes of our king. Medical reasoning has no effect on someone who believes that Jesus is stronger than cancer. They know He wants things on earth to look like they do in heaven and that He waits anxiously for us to speak His word to worldly situations, especially the "impossible" ones (Mark 11:22-24). People who understand the Father know faith unleashes the same power that created the world and raised Jesus from the dead. Compared to that power, the diseases or missing limbs don't seem like such a big deal. Seen through the eyes of Jesus, the toughest gangbanger becomes a hurting kid needing the love of our Father, and the dirtiest prostitute in the city transforms into a wayward bride craving affection and restoration.

Those are the eyes through which David and Barb see.

For the Sprays, it's not a question of if healing will take place, or whether it can. It's not a debate over whether or not God will show up, or even whether it's His will to do so. The question is over how God wants to do it, where, and when.

I've heard Dave tell people, "The Lord wants you healed. If you want to be healed, we can pray right now and it will happen for you."

I've listened as he and Barb lovingly taught the Scriptures, proving over and over that God really does want to make people whole in every way. "If you'll stand on this word and speak it," they say, "you just watch and see what God does for you."

David and Barb know their Daddy, and they have the same attitude as kids on the playground: "Our Dad can beat up your dad."

That's what makes David and Barb seem so audacious to the religious or unbelieving. They understand God's character.

They know He hates disease and sickness and pain (Psalm 103:1-5). They know He loves people, and they act accordingly.

What a novel concept!

Jesus calls believers to know God through intimacy with Him and to believe Him more than we believe the world. We must let Him change our viewpoint until we're just audacious enough to go to this broken world and proclaim, "The kingdom of heaven is here!" When the Sprays make that declaration, they don't hope to see miracles - they expect to see them.

What the world calls audacity, Jesus called boldness. Boldness doesn't back down, doesn't get its feelings hurt, and doesn't care who's watching. Arrogance focuses on self; boldness places the focus firmly on the cross, where one may behold the ultimate example of boldness. It ain't scared o' nothin', and no matter what happens, it proclaims, "Father, Your will be done!"

Boldness moves heaven, and when heaven moves, hell runs.

Scriptures for meditation:

Matthew 10:7-8
Romans 4:17
Psalm 103:1-5
Matthew 6: 9-14
Matthew 4:23-25

Make it real:

• Boldness vs. arrogance: boldness comes from being in love with Jesus. It is motivated by love for Him and comes from obedience. The result of boldness is glorification of Jesus. Arrogance comes from love of self. It is motivated by self-seeking and comes from the desire for glory. Arrogance results in the stern correction of the Lord. Ask the Lord to clarify and purify your motivation as you boldly proclaim the kingdom is at hand.

- Get a concordance or go online to look up the words for peace (Hebrew: shalom) and salvation (Greek: sozo, soteria). These definitions should make it clear that on the cross, Jesus bought not only eternal life, but prosperity (favor), protection, deliverance, and healing. He is also the Prince of Peace, meaning wellness, health, and completeness. I've heard this described as "nothing missing, nothing broken."

- Jesus taught us to pray that God's will be done on earth as it is in heaven. If it's not there, we have the right to pray that it be gone from here. If it is there, we have the right to ask that it also be here.

- When you feel the Lord provoke you to pray for the sick or broken, do so. Let the boldness of your love for Him move you to action. And even if you see nothing happen, **DO NOT STOP BELIEVING AND PRAYING!**

6

The Bedtime Dive

When I was younger, bedtime was an adventurous part of the daily routine. Typically, it involved a shower, which may or may not have included soap. Next came drying off, which consisted of standing in the vicinity of a towel for up to but not exceeding thirty seconds. After drying followed the possibility, but not the likelihood, of brushing teeth. Finally and most importantly, the evening concluded with the bedtime dive.

Imagine two little boys dripping wet from "drying off," charging from the bathroom in tidy whities. Hear the thunder of footsteps thum-thump-thumping down the hall. The thunder roars into the living room and ceases suddenly as the boys' feet effortlessly and gracelessly leave the floor. Time slows mid-air as two kids wearing only wide grins and Fruit-of-the-Looms hurtle toward their dad. Outwardly, Dad smiles with arms wide open.

Inwardly, he braces for impact.

Ka-boom! Perfect ten! Yet another brilliantly executed bedtime dive. The day is complete.

As you can imagine, my dad is a champ when it comes to loving his kids. For most of my life Dad's six-foot-two, three hundred pound frame has been synonymous with safety, love, and fun. Dad would do anything for my brother Tyler and me, and his steadfast endurance of the bedtime dive proves it!

Even though Dad was practically a giant compared to us, neither my brother nor I could ever have been described as small for our ages. I imagine my dad's experience of the bedtime dive closely mimics that of having a hundred pound brick dropped on one's chest and groin area. The main difference is that bricks do not have elbows and knees that consistently find their way into unfortunate areas. Tyler and I did!

But Dad never objected when the foot-thunder began. Nor did he ever shout warnings for us to be careful or watch where our knees went. He just received his nightly beating, hugged us to his massive chest, and wished us a good night.

This nightly event from my childhood wonderfully portrays a father's love. That time right before bed brimmed with intimacy and acceptance. It probably wasn't all that much fun for Dad, but he welcomed it anyway, and neither one of us ever had cause to doubt that he would allow it night after night.

It was like he was saying, "I'm giving you permission to hurt me because I know you don't mean to and because the chance to love on you means so much more to me than the little bit of pain it causes me."

And Dad never let the occurrences of the day discourage the bedtime dive. No matter what we had done that day or how much trouble we had been in, my brother and I could always count on that one last exhilarating leap onto our Daddy before bedtime. He loved it, too, because he loved us.

That sentiment so captures the heartbeat of our Father. God eagerly desires His kids to throw themselves unabashedly on His love. He's a great big Daddy with a great big lap, and He doesn't mind if we sometimes get a knee or an elbow in the wrong place. He just wants us to trust Him enough to jump.

"Don't worry," He says. "I will catch you. Jump!"

Still, so many people are afraid to make the leap. "He won't do that for me," they claim. "I just have too much sin."

Others believe they have to perform a certain number of prescribed tasks before they can dive. They believe God stands over them with a checklist of chores they must complete before they can come to Him. To some people, it has simply never occurred that God would want them to dive onto His chest. In their minds, God is simply too dignified or too holy to allow such nonsense!

Sadly enough, there are far too many people in this world who can't believe that God would invite them to dive onto His heart because to them, "father" means something or someone really bad.

Nevertheless, God, our fun-loving Father, has exposed His heart to us in such generosity and openness that many people can hardly believe, let alone understand it. His attention, His affection, and His love are focused on His kids with an intensity of devotion far above even the best of earthly dads. He yearns for His beloved children to turn to Him even for a second, and when they do, He falls even more in love with them. He calls them near to rest on Him.

"Just jump," He beckons. "I'm here and I want you to do it!"

But what will we find if we do jump?

My father's chest was a resting place, a refuge. Right there with him, no bad guy could harm me, no worry could touch me, and no fear could come near me. The only thing welcome in that place was the knowledge that everything was okay because Dad made it okay! That's what he did. He made things okay.

That is exactly what God wants His kids to realize. God made it okay for us to come. He did all the work so we would never have to earn the right to approach Him. Romans 5:1 says faith has justified us, given us peace with God, and granted us access to grace. God's grace beckons us near.

My dad never told me, "Clean up the bathroom and do fifty pushups. Then you can come jump on me." If he said anything like that, it would have sounded utterly ridiculous.

But many Christians labor under the lie that they need to do something before they have the right to come to God for rest and acceptance. The problem is that there is nothing left to do! All that needed to happen for us to come to God took place on the cross. Jesus tore the veil of separation and permanently opened a way for His kids to come.

It's like we're standing in a hallway, dripping in the blood that made it okay for us to sprint recklessly and joyfully down the hall toward God. Down at the other end awaits a throne room with the best Daddy there ever was, eyes twinkling with delight in his kids, arms wide open, waiting.

Any child in this situation would know exactly what to do. It's obvious.

Beloved, it's time for us to put down the guilt and shame and works for a little while. Time for rest waits just around the corner, but first, take a look at that awesome Daddy at the end of the hall. He's not angry. He has already forgiven you for everything that stops you from going to Him, and if you don't think He has, then all you have to do is ask.

It's time to forget dignity and fly down that hallway to the throne room like an eight year old in his underwear. It's time to leap dazzlingly into the air and crash into that warm bosom of grace.

It's time to just stay there for a moment and be held, completely free, completely safe. It's time for a blessing and for rest, knowing that Dad has made it all okay. It's time to take a deep breath and enjoy the moment.

And no matter what happens tomorrow, He'll still be right there waiting patiently for the next time we get ready for another dive.

Scriptures for meditation:

Romans 5:1-2
John 17:20-24
Song of Solomon 4:9
Colossians 1:19-22
Colossians 2:13-14
Psalm 32:8-9
Hebrews 10:11-25

Make it real:

• As you read in Hebrews 10:19-20, Jesus made it okay to come to the Father. His blood covers you. If you feel any resistance at all to your freedom to come to God in the Holiest place, plead the blood of Jesus and cry out to your Daddy.

• One practical way to draw near to God is to "soak" in His presence. Play worship music, or get somewhere quiet. It is best to sit or lie down so that you're completely still. Invite Holy Spirit to come and simply be with you. Turn your heart to Him and simply receive His love.

• As you practice soaking, remove distractions and don't set religious time limits or requirements. The purpose is to simply be with God. He may direct you to Scripture passages, give you instructions, or show you things. You may just lie or sit there for a while. That's all right. The point is to give Him your attention and affection.

• Ask God to show you how He reacts when you glance His way. Journal what you receive. (By the way, it's okay to ask multiple times.)

7

Ty-er Ty-er Man!

Dum-bada-dah! Whoosh!

A skinny-as-a-rope, blonde-headed little boy dashed into the room grinning wide enough to swallow a melon. He sported bright red underwear outside his blue body suit, which would have fit other kids tightly, but drooped from his tiny body. On his chest beamed a bright red "S," Superman style. A cape swung from his shoulders, fluttering impressively every time he darted from place to place.

He may have never struck fear into any villain worthy of that title, but in his own twinkling eyes, my brother Tyler, dressed up for Halloween, was the real Man of Steel!

This snaggle-toothed upstart looked more like a Little Rascal than a world saver, especially if you judged by his mischievous smile, but you would never have convinced him of that.

"Oh my goodness!" Mom exclaimed in that overly exaggerated voice of excitement that only mothers can somehow make to sound real. "It's Superman!"

Now you may think my brother would be delighted to be called that. You'd expect his face to beam even brighter as he zoomed around the room in a victory lap, but instead he furrowed his brow and crossed his skinny arms. The look on his face was that what-the-heck-are-you-talking-about expression all children perfect by the time they are four.

Mom was stricken, unsure of what she had said wrong. She was about to ask, but Tyler set the matter straight.

"Mine not Superman," he told her in a voice that was at once impatient and irritated. He made the name "Superman" sound like the equivalent of mashed green peas. Then he took a deep breath and boomed, "Mine TY-ER TY-ER MAN!"

Out came the grin and the victory lap ensued. Watch out mega-villains! A new superhero was on the prowl, ready to carry out justice, save the world, and defeat evil wherever it showed its ugly face. Ready and willing, that is, as long as it was before 8:30 because that was bedtime.

It is pretty easy to laugh at the notion of that skinny four-year-old saving the world, and trust me, we did. To this day, my family still refers to my brother, who recently finished medical school and has begun actually saving lives, as Ty-er Ty-er Man. These days, his name is Doctor Ty-er Ty-er Man, thank you very much.

And if you are anything like we were, it is probably fairly simple for you to laugh and dismiss my kid brother as harmless, silly at best. But if you stop and think about his heart for a second, you'd almost have to admire the kid.

For most of us, being like Superman is a dream so unattainable, you'd have to invent a new word to describe the unattainable-ness of it. Seriously, who wouldn't want to fly, to toss cars around with one hand, to shoot laser beams from our eyes, and to do all of that while saving a beautiful damsel in distress (or gentleman in duress, as the case may be)? Heck, I'd just like to know what it felt like to run fast enough to feel wind on my face. But to be like Superman? No way!

For my brother though, being like Superman just wasn't enough.

That scrawny little kid had the courage and the imagination to dream past his unimpressive-looking body and see someone even cooler that the man in blue tights. Superman? Pshaw! Why stop there when he could be so much more awesome? He could be Ty-er Ty-er Man! I can't help but admire someone who dared to see in himself a hero even greater than the greatest hero ever imagined.

Most of the rest of us, on the other hand, are much more like Gideon than my little brother. Rather than looking at ourselves with the eyes of hope and wonder, we stare into the mirror of shame and doubt, full of the judgments and disappointments life has dumped on us.

In chapter six of Judges, Gideon encountered an angel of the LORD. He was hiding in a winepress threshing wheat, hoping nobody found him. He didn't have much hope for himself other than to survive. He was completely alone. Then the angel showed up and proclaimed, "The LORD is with you, mighty man of valor!"

Though it's not told this way in the Scriptures, I can just imagine Gideon peering back over his shoulder, then glancing around the cellar, trying to figure out who in the world this crazy angel must be talking to. I can see him gathering up just enough courage to squeak out, "Who, me?"

He had just been called a mighty man of valor by the God of Hosts, and Gideon, just like most of us, could not believe it. His reply to the angel might as well have been, "I'm the biggest sissy in all Israel! I can't do what you're asking me to do!"

All of us have been in that place. God plants amazing dreams and desires in our hearts, yet we insist on telling Him why they will never come to pass.

"I'm too young."

"I'm too old."

"I don't know how."

"They won't like me if I do this."

"I'll probably mess it up."

"I'm not smart enough."

"I'm too smart." Imagine God chuckling at this one.

The list goes on and on. Some people have even built a

theology that claims that God just doesn't do miracles any more, that the time of empowered saints has passed.

Whatever the reason, many of us simply cannot look at ourselves and see the greatness God saw when He spent eons thinking of us before creation. While God spent an eternity before time crafting us with love and affection and preparing for us amazing works by which we could demonstrate His glory, we take one glance and dismiss ourselves. Yet our hearts yearn to be more than what we've been told we are. Deep inside, everyone longs to be heroic.

I think we would all do well to notice two things about the story of Gideon's calling. First, Gideon wasn't brave or mighty because of his muscles or his amazing faith. He wasn't gifted in wisdom, he probably wasn't exceptionally good-looking, and he certainly wasn't overflowing with courage. He simply was what God said he was.

One thing we learn from Genesis is that what God says, is! God says let there be light, and light is. God says divide the waters, and they are divided. You get the idea.

So if God said that Gideon was a mighty man of valor, he was. Right then, no matter what he had been, Gideon became a mighty man of valor not because he earned it or worked for it, but because God sovereignly declared it to be so. That is the power of the spoken prophetic word. What God says about us, we are, and we get the honor of walking it out.

So who does God say we are? He calls us wise, redeemed, sanctified, justified, kings, priests, sons, instruments of righteous, saints, and dearly beloved, just to name a few. The Bible is full of our identity as sons and daughters of God. And since God says this is who we are, then it is so, whether we like it or not!

Second, and more importantly, the angel told Gideon, "The LORD is with you."

What if you were called to do something and someone told you Superman would be with you to help you do it? Would you worry about your abilities or shortcomings? You'd probably not even think twice about saying yes because you had Superman with you. Wherever you failed, he'd take care of it for you. You'd be sure to succeed.

I don't mean to deride Superman or the creative people who invented him, but compared to God, Superman, or even the great Ty-er Ty-er Man are less than dust. Superman, even in fiction, never created a single thing. He never parted oceans, framed entire worlds, or raised the dead by commanding them to come forth. He certainly could not empower others to do the things he did. Jesus Christ does all of those things. Not only does He Himself walk in absolute power, but He promised everyone who believed in Him that they would do the things He did. Superman is cool, but Jesus is Lord.

So when God told Gideon, "I am with you," He was basically saying, "I am so great you will be great because of Me." He was not boasting; He was simply telling the truth. God took the self-proclaimed sissy of sissies and transformed him into a mighty warrior who defeated a vast army using only trumpets, pots, and torches.

Now that is a hero!

Today, Christians have something even better than Gideon because that very same God Almighty dwells within us. The One Who destroyed the Egyptian army fights through us. The One Who made Solomon the wisest of the wise lives in our thoughts. The One Whose resurrection power not only raised Jesus from the dead but also rescued us from damnation and death has now promised that we get to do what He did and even greater things!

Saints, we really are an army of superheroes, a host of Ty-er Ty-er Mans equipped with a power that really makes Superman look silly.

The only obstacle to that reality is a lack of faith. We must renounce the old identities and stop believing the lies of the world. We must be willing to let God show us the greatness and power he has intended for every single believer. We must remember that it does not depend on us but on God and our absolute surrender to Him. Then we will see what God intended all along. We will finally realize that we are all heroes sent to save the world, and not one of us is alone.

Let's take a lesson from a four-year-old in tights who dared to look inside himself and see a hero of the magnitude of Ty-er Ty-er Man. May we all find faith to gaze into our hearts and see Jesus.

Scriptures for meditation:

1 Corinthians 1:30-31
Romans 6:13
1 Peter 2:9-10
1 Corinthians 1: 4-9
Revelation 1:5-6

Make it real:

• Proverbs 23:7 says "As he thinks in his heart, so is he." As you read God's word, confess it over yourself. For example, "I am an instrument of righteousness. I do not present my members as instruments of unrighteousness, but to God as alive from the dead." Allow His word to change your thinking about yourself.

• Repent for any area in which you have not agreed with God's word. If He says you can do it, you can. Period.

• Remind yourself at all times that God is with you. Nothing is impossible for Him. You've got Somebody bigger and better than Superman with you all the time, and He'll never let you down.

Part Two: God Speaks My Language

Recently while I was soaking (lying in God's presence, worshipping), God showed me a picture of an old Winnie the Pooh bear I used to cuddle with when I was younger. At first, I thought my imagination had run away with me, but God insisted that I think about that old Pooh bear for a moment.

"God, why are you having me think about this?" I asked. He replied that the answer should be obvious. I thought about what that Pooh bear meant to me. It comforted me when I was little. It brought me peace. When I slept, I would cling to that little yellow bear in its red shirt as if my whole world were contained in it.

"You're that Pooh bear to me," the Lord whispered. "And I want to be that bear to you."

When God hid the mysteries of the kingdom, He hid them for us, not from us. He enjoys revealing the deep things of His heart, and He likes each and every one of us enough to do that for us. He doesn't just talk to the prophets and the big-wigs. He talks to the so-called "normal" people, too. Best of all, God is so clever He can put deep truth into a message we can understand.

He knows what we like, what we don't like, what we think about, and what we dream about. He's humble enough to use things from our own hearts and minds to form messages and meaning. Here are some things He's told me in words I understand.

8

Worth

I get a big kick out of these TV shows where people take their "priceless" antiques to an evaluator to find out how much they are worth. Apparently these folks miss the irony in their actions. They assure us it is only for curiosity's sake they do it, and they would never sell these heirlooms. Yet, their eyes light up when the evaluator informs them that the item is worth thousands of dollars. Suddenly, the prospect of selling the object doesn't seem so bad. It's really funny.

What's even funnier is that some of the things that are apparently worth a ton of money are things I wouldn't buy for a nickel. It's nice that your Aunt Molly's feather duster was apparently made by a famous French designer, but I don't want it. In fact, I wouldn't take it if you paid me. To you, it is a family heirloom that is beyond price. To me, it's worth nothing.

I once heard of an antique salesman who refused to put price tags on his items. He reasoned, "It is worth whatever somebody will pay for it, no more, no less." This man understood worth.

The best measure of what something is worth is what someone will give up in order to get it. Something truly is priceless when its owner would never give it up, and would not take anything for it. Likewise, something is priceless when the one who desires it would give up anything to get it.

With that in mind, let's shift our focus from objects to souls. At some time every person wonders, "What am I worth?"

We have established that something or someone is worth whatever someone else will give up to obtain them. So let's consider exactly what Jesus paid for us.

Imagine a place so pure that there is no darkness. Every object and every creature in this place radiates with pure light so that there is no blemish, no spot, no hint of anything unworthy or dark.

Imagine that this place is so wealthy that the streets are paved with gold. The gates are made of purest pearl. Walls are stacked twelve layers high made of precious stones. These stones, however, along with the gold and pearls have been so purified as to give the appearance of clear crystal. There is nothing hidden in this place. Everything knows perfectly and is perfectly known.

A sparklingly bright light, brighter than ten thousand suns, shines from the Ruler of this place in overwhelming power, yet does not hurt the eye to see. Everything in this place glimmers, and all things are made even more beautiful because of this pure and perfect light.

In such a place as we are imagining, all the treasures of our world would amount to a pile of dust, and would likely be discarded as such. This is a kingdom of wealth beyond wealth.

Now imagine the inhabitants of this kingdom. Imagine six-winged angels flying about here and there, singing songs and melodies so rich your heart literally beats out the rhythm to the song. There is never a wrong note, never a missed cue, never a pause in this music. The composition fills the air with joyous praise of the king of the realm.

Imagine that all the angels relate to one another in perfect servitude, never valuing one above another. Each willingly serves the others, and none is ever jealous or selfish.

Imagine varieties of angels the likes of which even the most creative artists have yet to consider. Angels abound of every size, color, and shape, each bearing its own responsibility in highest honor and joy, each with its special, perfect function that is vitally important to the thriving of the kingdom. This is a perfect kingdom in which all the subjects adore and honor their king, who adores and honors them.

Now imagine the ruler of this kingdom, God Most High. He is a kind and generous king who created each part of the kingdom with tender care. The variety of His creation demonstrates His attention to even the most minor detail. He fashioned this kingdom in perfection for the purpose of joy. He takes a profound joy in the things He has made, and He looks at each one with a special sense of fulfillment. This ruler chooses to express Himself in three parts: the Father, the Son, and the Holy Spirit. These three, who are one, relate in perfect love to each other and to all creation. None lacks, none hurts, and none is unsatisfied in any way.

Imagine that this entire kingdom, beasts, angels, and even the objects are all bent in pure adoration toward their awesome Lord and king. There are no bitter thoughts, no hurt feelings, and no plans to do anything but worship and glorify the Ruler who has created such a place with such opportunities. All love their king completely.

They never get hungry or sick. They never feel shame or pain of any kind. Fear does not exist. All these earthly elements are swallowed up in excitement and praise for the One who made it all, and for Whom it all is.

Even if you were just a servant in this place, it would be hard to imagine something you wanted so much you would leave your amazing home to go and seek it. Yet, our Redeemer Jesus did even more than that. He was the very ruler of this place. All of it and more than I can even describe belonged completely to Him. All of His possessions resonated with love for Him. He was the source of light that gave everything its glory, and it was Him to whom all the inhabitants of heaven longed to show their beauty.

All of His subjects worshipped Him in love all the time, singing His praise, working for His pleasure, desiring nothing but that He would smile and enjoy what they did for Him. And it was His highest pleasure to spend all His time enjoying what was His.

So let's not shortchange the Author of all the universe when it comes to considering our worth. He knew what was His. He knew all that He had. He knew Himself to be God. And He didn't trade just a part of what He owned. He gave it all.

You see, beloved, what happened in Bethlehem was far more than just a birth. It was the highest and most holy king taking on the form of a helpless baby. It was the source of light entering the realm of darkness. It was the ruler of angels making Himself subject to men. It was an honored and adored king taking up the scorn and shame of a servant. It was a perfect spirit putting on corruptible flesh. It was the owner of all good treasures giving all of it away for a broken, sinful, rebellious people who didn't even acknowledge Him as their Deliverer.

Jesus counted the cost, and He still paid the price. Even as He walked the earth, He was tempted by the enemy to take up His rightful position again, yet He willingly walked to the cross. At Golgotha, the glorious and omnipotent Lord of the universe subjected Himself to unbearable pain, allowed all the filth of the world to be placed on His body, and though He was and is the source of all life, gave Himself willingly to death.

Why would anyone do such things as Jesus did? None other than Jesus would. He chose to define His character as love. His uncompromising love made Him consider even the worst murderer in the darkest prison worth giving up all He had so that He might win that man back to Himself. Jesus calls His church His bride, and to Him nothing in the universe is worth more. He would pay anything to bring her home.

Beloved, this is the king we serve. He generously paid the highest price not only for the Mother Theresas or Pauls of the world, but for you. But there is even more to the story.

Let's rewind to the very dawn of creation. The enemy, through his crafty deceit, had tricked Adam and Eve, the beloved of God, into giving up their inheritance. Now, the only way the descendants of Adam and Eve could ever regain the inheritance of God was for a human to live a perfect life and give that life in their place. Only the holy king of creation could do it.

Jesus willingly came to accomplish the task. Remember that He was equal with God and if He were not perfected in love for the Father and for us, He could have refused. But Jesus Himself volunteered to come as He did.

Picture God the Father, Jesus, and Holy Spirit leaning intently forward over all creation, eagerly awaiting the day they could enact their plan to redeem fallen man. Together they watched until the day Father turned to Jesus and said, "Now, Son. Go bring them home."

And Jesus leapt up and ran to carry out what He had always desired: to give Himself for a spotless bride. Jesus knew He would suffer immensely, but He went anyway. Father God understood that He would have to watch His beloved Son be crucified, but He did not relent. Holy Spirit recognized that at the cross, He would have to leave Jesus alone, yet even that did not deter Him. The Holy Trinity made up their minds together, and they would stop at nothing to bring mankind home.

This is the worth God gives to every person who calls on His name. He gave everything He had for us. And nothing we do or say will ever change the price He paid. That, my friends, is what we're worth.

Scriptures for meditation:

Isaiah 6
Revelation 4
Revelation 19:11-16
Revelation 21:1 – 22:5
John 15:9

Make it real:

• As you read the descriptions of heaven in the Bible, realize that's what Jesus left behind for your sake. He loves you with perfect love. Your worth in His eyes is established, and it will never change. Your sin does not change the price He paid. Thank Him from your heart.

• Repent for any time you have agreed with lies about your worth. Speak the truth over yourself: "Jesus gave it all for me. He determines what I am worth, and He says I'm worth everything."

• Ask for a greater personal revelation of your importance to Jesus. Ask Holy Spirit to show you the height, width, depth, and length of His love for you.

9

Boots

Sometimes I think God is just messing with me. Seriously. I believe God shows me things sometimes just to see my raised eyebrow and puzzled expression as I try to sort out what He's doing. He's a Dad, right? So you know He enjoys giving His kids puzzles and watching them try to solve them.

God likes to use my imagination as puzzle material. Once, during worship, God sent me a flash of a giant champagne bottle being poured over the room. My mind started whirring.

"Okay, is He showing me that we're a wineskin?" I asked in my mind. "Is this an outpouring of His Spirit? What is He doing here?"

I think it's funny how I sometimes try to make obviously simple things into some giant spiritual revelation. God probably just grins and says, "Nope, try again, buddy."

On this particular occasion, He was simply showing me that He was pouring out joy. The speaker that night talked about the bride making herself ready for Jesus and how joyful an occasion a wedding was, let alone the wedding of the Lamb. A couple weeks later, a different speaker elaborated about how the joy of the Lord is our strength, how joy is one of our birthrights as a believer, and how joy shines even in the darkest of hours. Even in my personal time with God, He pointed me to book passages and Scriptures about joy.

"Remember the champagne, Kev?"

"Yeah, God, I think I'm finally getting it. You're talking to me about joy."

Ever wonder if angels slap their foreheads and yell out, "Duh!"? I bet the ones who follow me around do.

Still, I love how God uses my imagination to give me revelation. It is exciting, and it reminds me of the verse that says, "It is the glory of God to conceal a matter, But the glory of kings is to search out a matter" (Proverbs 25:2). God has hidden truth for us, not from us, and Jesus has made us a kingdom of priests. He gave us the honor and continual excitement of seeking the kingdom, wherever it may be.

And it's fun!

As I received revelation of God's majesty, I would often see myself on my face in a huge throne room. Towering above me was an enormous figure on a majestic stone throne. I could look up as far as I could see, and my eyesight only reached as far as God's mighty knees.

Many of my deepest prayers have been directed to God's knees. I don't think He minds.

One night, I was praying in that immense throne room when God decided to play with me. The weighty throne loomed as high as it ever had. The colossal, white-robed knees beckoned as welcomingly as knees can. The fear of the Lord gently nudged me to the ground in awe as I prayed.

Suddenly I noticed the giant feet sported cowboy boots. I'm not talking about the straightforward brown work boot variety, either. These were flaming red cowboy boots, the kind crazy high school kids tuck their jeans into when they go dancing (I'm hoping this is just a small town West Texas thing).

Though I was taken aback, I dismissed the image and went back to praying. When I looked again, the boots were gone. Now, the feet of the Most High rested in a pair of flip-flops.

"Really?" I thought to myself. "Come on Kevin, focus. You're supposed to be praying here!"

But the transformations didn't stop. I looked again, and now God's robe covered black, pleated khakis and penny loafers. These were followed by those old leather sandals people used to call "Jesus boots." Then came slippers, combat boots, and finally, what I considered most offensive and irreverent, a pair of pointy black stiletto heels.

At this point I opened my eyes and got up off the floor of my living room. I was pretty disappointed. Always before, when the Holy Spirit took my imagination to that throne room, I had experienced peace, or the immense weighty presence of God, or the fear of the Lord. Now my goofy flesh was showing me high heels. Leave it to me to mess up something perfectly spiritual.

Then God whispered, "Ever walked a mile in My shoes?"

I froze, stunned. He had asked me a simple question, but somehow I knew exactly what He meant.

We use that expression as an exhortation not to judge people without knowing their hearts. I grew up hearing it from my parents and teachers, especially when I had made some rude or unnecessary remark about someone.

"Don't judge someone until you walk a mile in their shoes!"

I don't mean to sound like Forrest Gump here, but you really can tell a lot about someone from their shoes. Shoes indicate occupation, social status, and style. They are one more form of expression that communicates a piece of who someone is. And to walk in someone's shoes would be to truly understand who they are, what they do, and what they like.

That evening, I was convicted because far too many times, I have withheld the living Word of God from people because I took one look at them and decided not to approach them. One of my ongoing excuses to the Lord was, "God, I don't think I have anything to say to that person. They're nothing at all like me."

You see, I'm a middle class, generic-looking, hair-parted-on-the-left white guy. I have no tattoos or piercings. Most hats make me look goofy, and that's okay, because I pretty much am goofy. I listen to Weird Al for fun, and I used to be able to quote most of the original three Star Wars movies in their entirety. What in the world do I have to say to the gothic kid at the supermarket, the biker who lives next to the supernatural training center I go to, or the old Mexican man struggling down the street with his cane?

There's really no question that believers are sent to the world the same way Jesus was. Jesus commanded us to preach the gospel to all creation, plain and simple. There's not much room for interpretation or questioning whether or not it is His will for me to tell people about Him. My problem was that I feared I would walk up to them and instantly be rejected.

In the vision I had, God wore the shoes of all kinds of people. He was showing me that He truly does understand every single person in this world. I may not be able to relate to the person I see somewhere out there, but Jesus can! Jesus had each individual person on His mind when He went to the cross. There was not a single one He left off, thinking, "Well old Joe, he just won't receive me, so no love for him." Jesus knew all of us, and He went to Calvary for the cowboy, the rocker, the nurse, the gangster, and the hooker. These folks are simply the bride to Him, and He desperately loves them, regardless of what I think of them.

And furthermore, who am I to decide that someone won't receive the gospel based on the way they look? Truthfully, I was more afraid of being shut down or shut out than I was passionate for someone to be touched by Jesus.

The gospel of Jesus Christ is not bound by status, wealth, poverty, occupation, or any of the social boundaries that separate people from those who are different. It is living and powerful to every city, every culture, and every individual to whom it is preached.

In the light of that solid fact, I had to repent for not believing in the power of the gospel that saved me.

What a sad statement to make. Yet, I am sure there are many more like me out there. There is definitely a need to repent and return to our first love. We must shift the focus off of ourselves and onto the very thing that transformed us from what we used to be into what we are now. And we must believe that the gospel is powerful enough to produce fruit, regardless of the audience and regardless of how well or poorly we share it.

God has walked in each person's shoes, and He loves them anyway. He knows how to talk to them, just like He knows how to talk to you and me. He's not scared, and He doesn't want us to be either.

It's cool to think that the Creator of the universe has walked in my shoes, too. He showed me that vision so I'd stop being scared and go have fun with Him. And maybe He likes the puzzled expressions on people's faces when His goofy son comes strolling up and starts up a conversation.

"Hey, nice shoes! Has anyone ever told you about Jesus?"

Scriptures for meditation:

Ezekiel 2:6-7
Ezekiel 3:16-21
Matthew 9:9-13
1 Corinthians 9:19-23
Hebrews 4:12-13

Make it real:

• Ask Holy Spirit to show you any people, people groups, or individuals you have judged. Renounce your judgments of them specifically, and repent to the Lord for judging them. Pray for those people to receive Jesus and His blessings.

• Ask God to fill you freshly with Holy Spirit, and specifically ask for words of knowledge or encouraging words for people you will encounter today.

• The gospel is powerful to every tongue, tribe, and nation. Ask for opportunities to share the gospel with someone soon. As you share, don't hold back.

• Claim the promise of Ezekiel 2: "Lord I shall speak your word, whether they receive it or not. I will not be afraid of their words, nor shall I be dismayed by their looks, in the name of Jesus."

10

Daddy God

What a delight to watch a daddy with his son. He teaches, he trains, he comforts, and he consoles. He rejoices and laughs, and he holds his son so tenderly. The love they share knows no limit or boundary. They are free to be and do according to the desires of their hearts. The son depends fully upon the father, and the daddy takes pleasure in bringing his child the highest good.

And to think: Jesus called God "Daddy." His whole life was a picture of the intimacy and power of sonship.

When Jesus was born, God sent angels to make the birth announcement and organized a baby shower from kings. Prophets rejoiced with God's heart when they saw Jesus, and the shepherds simply could not stop chattering with Holy Spirit about this One who had come. God threw a big party in heaven and told the world, "I like you so much, I'm sharing my Son with you!"

When the enemies of Jesus tried to exterminate Him, God stood guard as a watchful daddy. Through the night seasons, His eye never left His baby, and He moved Jesus quickly out of harm's way.

God clapped happily at Jesus's first step, listened intently to His first word, and watched excitedly as He explored the world

His Daddy had made for Him.

God taught Jesus diligently in the ways of heaven. Even at the age of 8, Jesus could put the teachers on their heels with His intimate knowledge of God. Can you just hear Him in the synagogue saying, "My Dad says…"? And as God watched and smiled, He thought, "That's my boy!"

God watched Jesus grow into a man. Jesus learned a difficult trade that required both strength and patience. As a carpenter before power tools existed, Jesus worked hard. His sweat dripped freely on the things He fashioned.

Jesus loved His family. He obeyed Joseph and Mary as a respectful son. Even on the cross, Jesus showed regard for His mother.

Jesus was a man's man, yet He was gentle and respectful. God raised Jesus well.

Then Jesus came into His destiny. God kicked off Jesus's coming out party by having Jesus humble Himself in baptism. "Let it be so, to fulfill all righteousness," Jesus said to John. And when Jesus came up out of the water, Holy Spirit came to celebrate with Him and a proud Daddy God thundered from the throne, "That's my Boy!"

Then God set Jesus up with a fierce trial against a strong opponent. But God wasn't scared for His son at all. He believed in Jesus, and He knew Jesus would triumph. When Jesus defeated Satan's temptations, God looked at the devil and said, "Told you so."

God cheered as Jesus walked on water. He marveled at the hardness of the people's hearts, but rejoiced that even the hardness didn't deter Jesus from loving them. God applauded as Jesus fed the thousands. He nudged the angels with His mighty elbow as the multitudes were taught, healed, and delivered. Leaning over and beaming, He told the angels, "That's my Boy!"

God even found Jesus a perfect Bride! "He'll love her," God said, "and she will certainly love Him." So God prepared her, adorned her, and grew her up for Jesus, all the while boasting to her of His dear Son.

"My child," He told her, "there is none like the One to Whom I give you."

And when her heart strayed, God understood why His precious Jesus wanted so badly to go after her, though it cost Him everything to rescue her. So He allowed Him to go, but it was not easy.

God Almighty had to watch as they stripped His little boy, beat Him unmercifully past recognition as a man, and disgraced Him. God sat still as Jesus hung naked and bleeding on the cross. He held clenched fists at His sides as demons mocked the true-hearted king. "They'll get theirs," God promised.

Even the sun, when it saw the indignant Daddy God, hid its face for shame. Then Jesus gave up His life and God, in His great grief, ripped the veil of separation clean in two from top to bottom, saying to the bride, "Look! Open your eyes and see! Look at Him! He has made you a way to come to Him! All of this was for you!"

For three days, God steamed, awaiting the appointed time, a heartbroken daddy.

And then God took His Son by the hand, lifted Him triumphantly out of death and Hades, and put Him on display in the highest place in the universe.

"Look everyone!" God exclaimed. "That's my Boy!"

And God was so pleased with Jesus, He gave Him all power, all authority, all honor, and all the saints once and for all. And He promised, "Son, I will not let anyone or anything take any of this from You forever."

So now God and Jesus and Holy Spirit conspire together for good, to bring Jesus's bride home. He made her a way to come, so God in His love for Jesus, works night and day on this special project with His Son.

"Let's make her beautiful for Jesus, Holy Spirit," God says, full of passion. "Let's get her ready for Him!"

And glancing to the throne where Jesus sits, full of glory and anticipation, waiting for the fulfillment of the times, God is once again filled with love and whispers, "That's my Boy!"

What a magnificent Daddy! He will stop at nothing for His beloved Son.

Beloved, Jesus taught His followers that God loves them just as He loves Jesus. We have a wonderful Daddy. He is willing and able to move heaven and earth for His beloved children, the bride He has chosen for His Son. He loves it when we laugh. He catches all our tears in the palms of His hands. He watches us intently and never takes His eyes off of us. He hears our voice in the night and delights to rescue us. He relishes the tender moments we share with Him. He disciplines, corrects, and trains so we can be just like Jesus, dearly beloved and fully pleasing Him.

He is preparing us for His Son, and He won't stop until He is finished. He's not angry. He's passionate about us because He's passionate about Jesus.

And just like the Daddy He is, God looks at us with the same love He has for Jesus and says, "That's my girl! That's my boy!"

Scriptures for meditation:

Revelation 21:9 – 21
Ephesians 5:22 – 33
Ezekiel 16
Isaiah 54
John 14:1-6

Make it real:

Jesus was a model for us in how to relate to God. He only did what He saw His father doing, and He only said what His Father said. He showed us how to live out of intimacy with God. He knew God as Daddy. He offers the same thing to believers today. Ask the Lord to heal you of any wounds your earthly father has put on you, and ask for a greater revelation of your relationship with God as a beloved child.

11

Champion King

Everyone dreams of becoming a champion. The prestige that accompanies that title pushes athletes, chess players, and academics to train vigorously. They must devote huge chunks of time and focus intently on the goal: becoming the number one winner in their arenas, the champion.

The word "champion," however, hasn't always meant the winner of a given competition. An older usage of the word referred to "the king's champion," a knight who volunteered his life to defend the honor and reign of his king.

In old British tradition, the king's Champion arrived at coronation ceremonies in full battle dress. He wore polished armor and carried his battle shield and his broadsword, among other weapons. As a part of the ceremony, he would throw down his gauntlet and issue a challenge: anyone who had a problem with the new king's place on the throne could come and meet the king's Champion in combat to the death.

According to the Encyclopedia Britannica, the king's Champion only had to fight twice in all history, and even one of those occurrences is not confirmed. That's not surprising, even in times when duels were more common. Someone passionate enough to forfeit his life will not likely encounter many who feel as strongly as he does.

Jesus called that kind of passion the greatest form of love, and that type of love is undefeatable.

Believers have the privilege of being appointed king's Champions for the king of all kings. He calls upon us to represent Him in this dark world, to throw down our gauntlets in the presence of principalities and powers and all other forces of darkness that would oppose His reign, and to wage war on His behalf (Ephesians 6:12).

He has given us His passion for the kingdom of heaven, and our zeal for the rightful king propels us to say, "Here I am! If you have a problem with Jesus, you have a problem with me!"

He has clothed us in spiritual armor and entrusted us with the sword of the Spirit, His very word. God has assigned legions of angels to each of us to help win the battle. As king's Champions, we duel sickness, step on the throat of demons, and even battle death itself in the name of the king! Our battle cry is "Repent, for the kingdom of heaven is at hand!" Our rallying point is the love of our God. We never retreat; we never back down.

Our king always wins!

And leave it to this beautiful king to do even more than give us the honor of being His champions. He has not only appointed His saints to the position of Champion, He Himself has become Champion for us.

An even older use of the word "champion" comes from a Germanic law tradition called "trial by combat." Trial by combat was basically a duel in which the winner was considered the correct party. Imagine suing someone and deciding the outcome by a fistfight. That's how trial by combat worked, except it involved a fight to the death. Whoever lived won the verdict.

One stipulation in this form of trial allowed those unable to fight fairly to choose a champion. The sick, the handicapped, the elderly, women, and children who were accused or sued could select someone to fight in their place in the trial by combat. The champion would need the strong conviction that the principles involved justified the party for which he fought, making him a champion of the cause.

Or perhaps he loved them enough to risk his life to defend theirs.

The accuser of the brethren loves accusing us to our Father, to our brothers and sisters, and even to ourselves. He scoops up our nasty sin and pushes it in our face.

"You're guilty," he snarls, "and I challenge you to prove otherwise."

The devil is a coward, and he only challenges us because he knows he's bigger, older, and stronger than we are by ourselves. He lures us into battle by bringing the accusation and making us feel that we must accept the challenge of proving our innocence. So we try to counter his accusation with the list of the good deeds we've done. We defend our good intentions, laying out the perfect case and proving that our downfalls were merely accidents. We insist that we're basically good and therefore could be considered innocent.

But the devil knows the law, and he knows one single unforgiven sin makes us undeniably guilty. In this trial by combat, our enemy can annihilate us every time. Imagine Tiny Tim entering the ring against the UFC heavyweight champion, and you have a good picture of what this fight looks like. We lose.

Jesus, however, loves to make things new, and He turned the tables on the adversary. On the cross, Jesus gave us the right to acknowledge that we're too weak to enter this contest, and we are unable to withstand this enemy. Rather than fight ourselves, Christians have the right to select a champion. In our place stands the undefeated, undisputed, heavyweight champion of the universe, King Jesus.

When the accuser slaps us in the face with his accusations, we no longer accept the challenge. We call on our Champion king. The Bible says Jesus disarmed our enemy, removing his weapons (Colossians 2:15). He shattered sin and defeated death. Temptation has no hooks in Him. He enters the ring a mighty, victorious warrior and stares at His opponent, who now looks not like a powerful foe, but more like a naked, shivering wimp.

That's the truth the accuser hates. When Christians acknowledge our guilt, confess our sin, and call on our Champion king Jesus, we are automatically judged innocent. We have a champion who has never lost a fight. He believes not only in the cause of the kingdom, but He loves us enough to stand in our place every time. He never tires of the battle. Rather, each time He defends His bride, He displays His valiant love for her.

"She's innocent!" He proclaims, sword raised and eyes aflame. "Anyone who says otherwise may challenge Me."

He tosses down His gauntlet in the face of the hosts of darkness, and not a one dares accept the challenge. Jesus knows what a million demon knees knocking together sound like. When none steps forward, He collects His prize and carries her back to where she belongs. He restores her righteousness and flies His banner of love over her.

What an amazing Lord we serve! He has granted us the honor of being His king's Champions. And when the enemy shows up to take us out, He has offered us His eternal service as our Champion king. We are His, and He is ours, just as He always intended.

Scriptures for meditation:
Colossians 2:13-15
Ephesians 6:10-18
Revelation 19:11-16
2 Corinthians 10 3-6
1 Peter 2:24

Make it real:

• As king's Champion, you represent Jesus on this earth. Your most effective defense of your king comes in your daily life. Your words, your actions, and your open witness will either defend or deny the reign of King Jesus.

• As Champion king, Jesus paid for our sins. He has rescued us from the power of sin and the accusations of the enemy. If there are any areas of sin with which you struggle consistently or for which you feel guilty, seek help from a mature believer in receiving your deliverance. Repentance is key.

• Jesus Himself defends you in your weakest hour. You're never alone. He sent Holy Spirit as comforter, counselor, and Lord. Cry out to God and He will hear and answer from heaven. Give the fight to Jesus, for He can and will win it on your behalf.

• Worship is key. Worship will help you encounter this champion of yours, and it will prepare you to live as a champion for Him. Worship every day in an attitude of thanks and adoration.

12

Talents

Imagine Jesus walked up to you and handed you $1,000. Your only instructions were that you must use that money to make Him look good.

Do you think you'd be just a little excited? I bet your imagination is starting to spin as you think of the different ways you'd put a thousand bucks to use for Jesus. There are tons of homeless in any city of any size who could eat for a year off that much money. Then there's the widow who could use some house repairs. Or what about the people who would take so much joy or encouragement from being given simple gifts?

You could do so much good with that money. You'd produce buckets of gladness, and your own heart would fill with love as you told each person, "This was actually a gift from Jesus. He told me to use this money to bless you."

Whatever you did with that money, it would satisfy your soul like a steak satisfies a starving man. You would have the honor of spending the king's money and the double honor of telling people how generous and good He was.

That's called "stewardship."

Stewardship means that someone takes care of someone else's property, managing it in ways consistent with the owner's character and desires. A steward has the full authority of the owner to do business, issue orders, and run the account or estate, yet the steward actually does not own any of it.

In older times, stewards were typically highly trusted servants or employees. A lord or lady may have owned several estates in several places. Therefore, he or she couldn't personally manage every place at once. Or perhaps the actual owner of an estate had not yet reached the legal age at which he or she could run things. In this case, an appointed steward took care of the property until the rightful owner came of age.

Property holders would train stewards rigorously in all the details that went into managing the servants, the land, and the resources of the domain. Only the most trustworthy could become stewards of their masters' territory. Furthermore, only the ones who most closely reflected their masters' character and who had the most favor could hope to maintain that prestigious office. To be a steward showed the trust and confidence of the true lord of the land.

Similarly, Christians consider ourselves stewards of all we have. All the earth rightfully belongs to our king Jesus, yet he entrusts each of us with a portion of it. Our job is to take care of it, grow it, and conduct business with it in a manner that pleases Him.

That sounds simple enough, right?

Most people who have attended church any length of time have been taught these exact lessons more times than they care to recount. However, a huge number of God's people still struggle with giving.

Giving seems hard because we no longer have the thing we gave away. Whether we give money, objects, food, or time, whatever we gave is no longer ours. That's a hard thing for humans to accept because we sow many times expecting nothing in return. That's not what Jesus taught. Jesus said that when we give, His blessing will overtake us, pressed down, shaken together, and overflowing (Luke 6:38). That makes it easier for us to let go. On top of that, God actually intended the act of giving to produce joy, not only in His heart, but in ours as well.

The parable of the talents illustrates why in the kingdom giving is as necessary as breathing.

The parable describes three stewards, each of whom received a portion of their master's possessions to oversee in his absence. Two of the three invested wisely, while the third foolishly buried his talent in the dirt. When the master returned, he generously rewarded the two who made gains, and took away even the small piece of his possession from the servant who did not gain.

Now you may judge the master as mean because he took away what the last servant had. But would you trust someone with your money if they had grossly misjudged your character and failed to do business the way you taught them to? I didn't think so.

The third steward believed his master to be a hard man. He misjudged the very one who trusted him enough to give him a piece of the kingdom. Rather than recognize the opportunity to please his lord, the third steward succumbed to fear and did the exact thing his master would not have approved. He buried what his master intended for him to multiply.

Conversely, the two stewards who knew the character of their master understood that he wanted them to increase his dominion. He didn't just want them to sit on it; he wanted them to exercise it. You can almost hear him telling them, "Now fellas, I've taught you what to do and how I do it. Now you get to do it." These two stewards risked losing what the lord of the land had given them, yet even if they had lost it, the ruler would likely have been pleased with their efforts to conduct business the way he did. Since they proved their trustworthiness to him, and since they showed they knew his heart, he gave them incredibly more than what they started with. They got to rule a piece of his domain, and they entered his joy.

That's the saddest part of the parable for the third steward. He missed out on his master's joy because of his fear. How many of us could say the same thing?

Fear always opposes generosity because generosity is one of the watermarks of genuine love. That's why grandparents are such pushovers. Grandpa was smitten with his little granddaughter the minute she was born, so he has no problem paying her twenty bucks to take the trash out. He wanted to give her that money, whether she did anything or not. Someone in love doesn't haul out the calculator and the ledger when an opportunity to give comes up. They just give.

But when we feel our Lord calling us to give, fear stands in the moment of decision and whispers, "What about you? What if you can't pay your bills because you give? What if you miss out on time with your family because you serve? What if this is not God's will? Won't He be angry with you?"

When we listen to that voice, giving becomes a scary proposition.

Our God loves a cheerful giver. God adores the one who can give something away with a sparkly smile. He dances when His children take the gifts He pours out and share them with others. More than that, He likes the opportunity to give even more.

God has poured His blessing out on the Bride. We're bristling with talent, skills, and assets we've received from the king of the universe. Jesus trusts us with these things! Our instructions are to steward whatever we have so that He takes pleasure in how we do it. He is training us to be like Him, showing us His will, and teaching us how to live the way He would. Freely we received; freely we give.

Best of all, this kind of stewardship multiplies the joy of our Lord.

In the beginning, God blessed mankind with the command to be fruitful, multiply, and spread His dominion over the whole earth. He didn't say, "Hold on to this until I get back." He said, "Take this and make more of it."

On the cross, Jesus restored this mission to all of His people. Our job is and has always been to receive the blessing of the Lord, bear fruit, and multiply his dominion so that it spreads over the entire planet. And when we do that, God grins.

But you don't spread dominion by sitting on it. Just like the first stewards, we have to take risks, believing in the character of our God, and trusting in His forgiveness and correction. He cares more about our hearts being submitted to Him than He does about the final outcome. He's not worried.

God's a lot like that grandpa. God wants to give us blessings, whether we do anything or not. Yet, when we act like Him and pass that blessing around, that proves He can trust us. He's so proud He gives us even more. Then, we get to bless even more. It's a giant cycle of blessing!

Another way of looking at it is to consider yourself a kingdom investor. You have the capital of heaven, and your job is to invest that capital on behalf of Jesus. Everywhere you go, you spend your budget the way your CEO Jesus would, and you get to tell people how awesome He is because it's His money! Your investments automatically make gains for the kingdom, and Jesus pays out dividends regularly, so your own account grows, too!

I don't know about you, but that sounds like an awesome job to me. And that's the job we have in this kingdom. Whatever our talents or possessions, they came from the king, and we use them according to His desires. Even our time on this earth is from Jesus, and the time we take to listen or just be there for someone in His name produces fruit. And best of all, it is fun. Who doesn't take joy from knowing Jesus is pleased? Who wouldn't jump at opportunities to make Jesus happy and advertise for Him in this world?

Jesus said that whatever we do to the least in this world, He considers it done to Himself. Every time we give what we have, we're lavishing gifts on our king, and we bask in the glow of His pleasure. Besides, He already paid for it all, anyway.

Scriptures for meditation:

Genesis 1:26-28
Malachi 3:8-12

Genesis 22:15-19 (Abraham's stewardship of his son and God's promise in return)
Matthew 25:14-30
2 Corinthians 9:6-15

Make it real:

Tithes and offerings are not optional for Christians. As you read the Scriptures listed, notice that God blesses joyful givers, but a curse comes from withholding tithes. God tests our hearts toward Him in how we steward not only our finances, but everything we've been given. Remember Jesus' command: Freely you have received; freely give. Something that may help you is to think of your giving as giving straight to Jesus. If Jesus were standing in front of you, what would you withhold from Him?

13

Prodigal

It's really easy to look at what someone in the Bible says or does and think of all the ways I'd do it better, faster, or just look better doing it. Take, for example, Adam. Sometimes I just feel like asking him, "Adam, dude, what in the world were you thinking?"

I like to fancy that, given the choice between eternal bliss in Eden and death, I'd pick the happy ending. Surely I'm smart enough to choose life over destruction.

Or what about Peter? He promised Jesus he would never deny Him, but a couple pages later, good old Peter chickens-out in front of a little girl, no less. Come on, bro!

Times like that are typically when God reminds me that I would have done exactly the same thing. Probably worse.

The parable of the prodigal son is yet another passage I've read with critical eyes. It's easy for me to consider myself better than that poor sap who thought riches and pleasure would satisfy him. I can't help feeling wiser than he was. God smirks at that sentiment. The humbling truth is whatever wisdom I have, or for that matter anything I have, I received from Him. God developed it for me, He gave it to me, and He directs me in how to use it.

And that lesson is one the parable demonstrates full well.

The story is about a father welcoming home his rebellious son. It is about God rejoicing when a sinner comes into the kingdom. It is about mercy, forgiveness, repentance, and acceptance. The story shows that all the blessings of the Father are available to those who are with Him, and it emphasizes the importance of staying inside the protection, love, and authority of Jesus.

As the tale begins, the prodigal goes to his father and demands his inheritance. How did that inheritance come into being? It was through the hard work, planning, and goodness of the father that it even existed in the first place. The father had built up this inheritance for his son, eagerly awaiting the day he would give it to the boy. The son, however, did not trust the intentions of his dad, and demanded it that very moment.

In the same way, we believe that God has been saving up blessings for us since before time began. All of God's plans for us result in hope and a brighter future. We know God has an inheritance for us that He will always provide at the right time and in the right way. Yet many of us continually say to God, "Give it to me now!"

God knows best how, when, and where to give what He has stored up for His children. His people must learn to trust Him as we wait.

One sign of maturity is the ability to trust God fully without having received the things for which one hopes. A mature Christian recognizes the molding and preparation that accompany the waiting period, and he does not lose hope. Maturity comes from being with God, learning His character, and waiting patiently on Him.

Sometimes the purpose of the delay is to produce the character God wants in those He blesses. It's a well-known fact that we become more like the people with whom we spend time. Yet, like the prodigal, many of us mistake waiting for lack, so we miss out on the opportunity to become more like our Father as we wait for our inheritance. Because we haven't trusted fully in His good intentions for us, we fail to develop the character necessary to maintain and multiply what He gives.

In the next pivotal part of the story, the prodigal takes his inheritance and goes away. He leaves the father behind and removes his possessions from the supervision and authority of the one who built it.

The father had wisdom regarding the wealth. He knew how to store up and how to give. He knew how to maintain. He was motivated by love for his family, and he would have willingly taught his sons how to multiply themselves. However, in order for him to instruct them, they would have to remain in intimate relationship with him, obeying his instructions.

If someone wanted to give me an empire, I would want to stay and let that person show me how to build it, how to run it, and how to do the same for others. I have no clue how to generate and pass on empires. But I bet the person who built the first one could show me.

Imagine for a moment what might have happened had the son in the story asked for his inheritance, received it, and stayed with his father. How much wealthier would he have become with his father to teach him how to increase his possessions? What height might his social status have reached as he became a master like his old man? What counsel from the father may have averted the devastation that eventually overtook the son?

The young man in the story missed an amazing opportunity when he took his empire and went away, using it how he saw fit. The end result was utter ruin and humiliation. He didn't know how to maintain the wealth he was given. Outside the father's instruction and care, he came to destruction and despair.

The fate of the prodigal illustrates that whatever you take outside the Father's authority and reign dies. In John 15:5, Jesus taught the principle by saying, "Apart from Me, you can do nothing!" A lot of people I know describe the importance of giving and tithing the same way by saying, "You can have some of your wealth blessed, or all of it cursed!"

Any way you look at it, the root cause of the son's destruction was taking his inheritance away from his father. True, the sinful lifestyle he chose added to his downfall, but even that choice began when the son left the father and went his own way. Enticed by fleshly desires, the son disconnected his heart from the one who blessed him, pursuing instead the things that would destroy him.

It would be pretty easy to leave the story right there and say to the prodigal, "Yep, you got what you deserved. You should have stayed with your daddy, and you could have been blessed!"

But friends, all of us can identify with the need for forgiveness and restoration. Thank God He is the kind of Daddy who freely offers us those things every time we need it. But we can't define "prodigal" as simply one in need of forgiveness. In this parable, God highlights that any area of our lives outside of His rule and authority constitutes prodigality.

Do not make the mistake of limiting the scope of the story to wealth and sin. We know that our inheritance from God is in redemption, in godliness, in true wealth of love, and in many things for which we don't even have a measure. Our spouses are part of our inheritance, along with our children, our churches or Christian families, and our righteousness.

If we look at our inheritance in this light, we can see that every single one of us has at least something operating in a prodigal state. We have taken it out from under God's lordship. We think we know better. We think we can hide it. Or we may even be ignorant of God's intended purpose for that specific thing. Nevertheless, as long as it is outside God's rule, and therefore His protection, it is subject to the same ruin and humiliation that befell the prodigal son.

A couple years back, I made a financial decision in direct opposition to God's word. I thought my resources and my cleverness would keep me from trouble. I trusted the people involved, and I believed things would work out all right.

They didn't.

I found myself in debt. I had payments my salary would simply not support. Every month, I felt like I was flushing $600 down the toilet. Shame burned me, and frustrations over my situation mounted. I stopped tithing because I needed that money for other things. I had become prodigal by disobeying my Father.

After a while, Holy Spirit convicted my heart, reminding me of God's promises regarding giving to Him. Though I had to change my lifestyle, I began tithing again. My debt diminished, and surprise blessings started popping up. Suddenly, people were inviting me to movies and dinner and picking up the bill. At the beginning of the year 2009, God moved me to give Him my entire first month's paycheck.

Now I wish I could tell you I simply obeyed with joy. Instead, I got out my calculator and frantically planned out how I would survive for the next months if I gave that paycheck away. Nevertheless, I wrote the check with sweating palms and dropped it into the offering basket.

Now I'm not trying to tell you that if you give money to God, your life will be perfect in every way. But I do believe in the blessing of Malachi 3, and I know God honors a faithful heart. That said, 2009 was one of the best years of my life so far. I went through personal deliverance the likes of which I had never seen. I paid off all my debt. I began to accelerate in spiritual growth, and I even met the love of my life. When I turned back to my Father in love and obedience, He tackled me with blessing.

That's why the end to the prodigal's story is so beautiful. As many before me have taught, the father saw the son a long way off and ran to him. It was a long, undignified sprint that showed the father's watchfulness and love in greeting a returning child. It was a passionate embrace between a dumbfounded rebel and a merciful dad. It was extravagance in motion as love poured freely from the father's heart. It was a portrait of restoration.

The father didn't scold the son or nag him. He gave the ingrate gifts! The prodigal's father gave him a ring and a beautiful robe. These gifts symbolize the spiritual restoration Jesus offers.

First, the father gave his son a ring, which represents love. In weddings, the bride and groom give rings as a sign of covenant. Similarly, the father reminded the son through the ring that they were in covenant and the father's blessings were still in effect.

Promises depend on the character of the one making the promise, not on the actions of the one to whom promises are made. That's why God's promises never fail. He is faithful when we are faithless.

The ring is also a symbol of authority. Nobles in the past sealed letters with the imprint of their personal rings, which carried the same power as their signatures. The bearer of such a ring also carried the authority of the one who gave it. All he had to do was show the ring, and, regardless of his actual rank, the ring bearer would be obeyed as if he were the noble himself. Similarly, in giving his son the ring, the father was not only reaffirming his love for the returning one, but restoring his rightful authority as a son of the house.

Next, the father commanded the best robe to be brought. The robe symbolizes righteousness. By dressing the son in the best garb, the father was showing everyone that the son's rightful position was restored. Also, the robe reminds us of the time when people were clothed only in God's glory. Remember how in Eden, Adam and Eve were naked but not ashamed? That's because they were covered entirely in God's glory. God has never stopped desiring to clothe His people in His glory, and the prodigal's robe may very well symbolize the restoring of the glory covering.

Finally, the father ordered a celebration. The son expected a cold shoulder and a begrudged place among the servants. Perhaps he expected that treatment because we tend to judge others by what is in our own hearts. The father, however, was not like his son in this regard because the father was motivated by love.

Love forgives all things and is kind. The father's love made him more than willing to demonstrate his generosity to his son. In his joy, the father took the very things he had been saving for his son (which his son had demanded and squandered) and gave them freely. What a generous dad! There was no probation period, no point system, and no chart with stars to be earned. It was just a loving dad pouring out his heart on behalf of the son he never stopped loving. Now that makes a great party!

So I hope by now you're hearing the invitation to allow

Holy Spirit to point out the areas of prodigality in your life. We must all admit where we have wrestled control away from God and squandered the inheritance. We must face the fact that apart from the lordship of Jesus, we are ruined! That's the bad part.

The good part is that the act of surrender causes God's heart to rejoice. He rejoices in restoring to us righteousness and authority. He rejoices in proving yet again that His love has never failed, nor ever will. And He rejoices in taking the very thing we tried to remove from Him and giving it to us just because He can!

When we take things from the oversight of Father God, He stands watching and waiting for us to simply turn His way. When we recognize the broken and sad state things are in without Him, we can't help but want to return. And though our hearts would condemn us to servant-hood and penitence, God's loving response is to give us a beautiful ring, wrap us in a wonderful robe, and throw us a jubilant party.

We don't have to come back, we get to come back. We get to give it all to Him, and we get to watch His blessing cause us to multiply. And when it comes to our inheritance from God, multiplication is a good thing!

Scriptures for meditation:

Luke 15:11-24
Jeremiah 32:40
Jeremiah 33:19-26
Malachi 3:8-12
1 Corinthians 1:9
2 Timothy 2:13

Make it real:

• Repentance is a gift. It can hurt sometimes, but God allows us to repent so that His blessing can return to us. Repentance produces fruit. Repentance – leaving behind the prodigality and returning to the blessing – defeats sin and temptation and calls forth God's generosity toward us. He just wants us to turn to Him!

• Yep, you guessed it. Time to ask Holy Spirit to reveal what parts of your life are operating in prodigality. REPENT! Do it no matter how long it takes or how much it hurts. Be honest with yourself and with Him. Nothing is hidden from His eyes.

• Once you've repented, receive God's blessings of restored and increased love, righteousness, and your right to carry His authority.

• Pray something like this: "Father, in the name of Jesus I decree that my righteousness is restored because of Jesus' blood and your faithfulness to me. Your love never fails. Your character does not change, so Your blessings and promises to me are still in effect. I receive them now in Jesus' name. Restore love to me. Restore my righteousness according to your Word. Restore my authority as your son/daughter. I give you all areas of my life freely, and I submit to your rule. Teach me, train me, discipline me, and multiply me according to your will. In Jesus name, AMEN!"

14

Jericho

One of God's greatest gifts is the ability to dream. He planted desires, goals, and visions in our hearts as a source of hope, a wellspring of perseverance.

A person's dreams give him the motivation to fight one more round, to live one more day with the belief that tomorrow will be better than today. Every person has at some time felt he could improve some piece of the world, and whether he knew it or not, he was absolutely right.

In some ways, a dream is evidence of things not seen and proof of things hoped for. Dreams help build faith to call on God for things that may not yet exist. Yet, wherever there is a dream, especially a kingdom dream, there will also be opposition.

One of the most common and most insidious attacks the enemy throws in the face of believers is the statement, "It's never been done." No matter what your dream is, someone will pop up to tell you how impossible it is.

"Nobody has ever succeeded in building a church there."

"No one has ever gotten Ted to listen to the gospel!"

"You couldn't possibly reach that people group."

"Nobody from this town has ever had a full-time music ministry."

The voices are innumerable, bearing poison with hidden

effects. Sometimes dreamers overcome the poison and reach out in faith. Sometimes, the poison seeps through to the heart and destroys what truly was a beautiful dream.

There will never be an end to the scoffers and their scoffing. Until Jesus comes back, there will always be someone standing by watching the work of the kingdom and making fun of it. They snort and chuckle and talk about how silly it looks, how ridiculous it is to think the task is even possible, and how stupid you are to attempt it. They did it to Noah, they did it to David, and they did it to Jesus Himself. They will most certainly do it to you.

Many times, people give up because they start agreeing with the detractors. The task looks too big, the resources just aren't there, or God just hasn't seemed to show up yet. Then, the enemy turns up the scoffing with the goal of shutting down the dream. Far too often, that's exactly what happens.

But kingdom dreamers must never forget that what God says will happen always happens.

The Lord proved that indisputable fact in the story of the fall of Jericho. He showed us that He can do anything He wants, and He can do it however He chooses. The key is our obedience in the face of disparagement.

Many people have taught or written about Jericho already, and I'm not trying to change or contradict what they've said. I do, however, want to point out that many people who teach about Jericho focus on insurmountable nature of the wall. They ask, "What gave the Israelites faith to continue in the face of such a huge obstacle?" That's a perfectly valid question with answers that encourage faith.

But when I think about this story, I have to ask, "Why did the people of Jericho stay in the city?"

After all, this was not the first strong city with a mighty wall the God of Israel had knocked down. Chapters two and three of Deuteronomy detail a fairly substantial list of cities with huge walls of which the Israelites said, "We utterly destroyed them." Put in modern day sports terms, Israel and their Mighty God had delivered a series of over sixty consecutive forty-two-to-nothing beat-downs of every city that had attempted to withstand them by the time they arrived at Jericho. By any measure, 60-0 is an impressive record.

So why did the people of Jericho not flee in terror when Israel came knocking at their gates? They had to have been the most arrogant people who had ever lived. I can almost hear them talking.

"Well, those other cities may have fallen, but this city will never be taken!"

"Let the Israelites come. We've built a wall that nobody can climb, and nobody will ever enter our city until we give them permission."

"Conquer us? How could they possibly think to defeat us? It has never been done."

Imagine being in the army of Israel as they marched through the scorching desert on the way to the land God had promised. Your armor is heavy, your clothes are sweaty, and you haven't had a decent bath in recent memory. Suddenly, your commander points out the next city you're going to take, and it's Jericho.

Jericho's fame had spread throughout the region. It was impenetrable by human hands, and had withstood sieges from every army that had ever attempted to overtake it. It was probably visible from miles away. Joshua knew that God had given Jericho into Israel's hands, but I imagine there were plenty of eyebrow raising and head scratching as the soldiers observed the wall.

There were probably even more signs of confusion as Joshua unveiled the divine plan to take the city: "We're going to walk around it for seven days. Then we're going to shout."

Terrific.

I imagine that for six days, the nation of Israel put up with taunts, insults, and most likely some flying objects I don't care to think about. How many times did some yahoo lean over the walls to remind them that Jericho had never been defeated? Day after day, the Israelites marched around the same impenetrable wall listening as they were mercilessly mocked.

It would have been really easy for them to give up or complain, but they kept going. They knew something that drives the enemy nuts: when God's people obey Him, stuff happens.

For six days, though, it must have seemed like nothing would happen. On day seven, the scoffers got what was coming to them. The walls tumbled down and the people of God were once again victorious. Surprise!

I love that God chose the seven day march and the blowing of trumpets to take down Jericho's walls. The symbolic statements about carrying His mighty presence into the battle, about the praise of God as warfare, and about the power of passionate worship inspire me.

However, God could have chosen any way He wanted for the people to defeat Jericho, and the result would have remained the same. He could have told them to blow raspberries in the direction of the city and slaughter the soldiers as they came out to shut them up. He could have told them to all spit into the air and drown out the enemy. He could have just said, "You guys all sit down and watch Me incinerate this place." It wouldn't have mattered.

What matters is that God puts His glory on display for those who obey Him. Those who oppose His vision and His move are always buried under the rubble. Just as the obedience of Israel prompted the power of God, the obedience of modern saints will result in the same victory.

We must remember the importance of obedience. As I said, God could have chosen any way He wanted to destroy Jericho. For that matter, He could have done any number of things to save the world with Noah or deliver Israel from Egypt. He's God; He can do what He wants however He wants to do it. But God loves obedience, which Jesus taught is one of the greatest expressions of love. In all of history, He has continually taught His children to obey Him, regardless of what people will say.

And we all know they're going to say something!

It is easy to get discouraged when the scoffers start

chattering if we forget who our God is and if we forget that He always keeps His promises. No matter what the call or command may be, the most important task is to remember that God is God, and there is none like Him. He never fails, and He never backs down. He never leaves us nor forsakes us. It doesn't matter if the assignment has never been done. God can do it. He's giving us the chance to obey Him and the honor to see Him act on our behalf.

That's what encouraged Israel to keep walking in spite of the taunts from Jericho. They knew their God. This was a generation purged from the complainers and doubters who tempted God in the desert. This was an army who told the story of the Red Sea crashing down on Pharaoh. They remembered God's faithfulness to Abraham. They could draw pictures of the fire by night and the cloud of smoke by day. Oh, yes, and they had plenty of stories about walls their God had utterly destroyed.

So take this encouragement the next time something burns in your heart and all you hear is, "Well I just don't think it can be done." That is probably one of the best signs that God is about to move. After all, if someone has already done it, why would He still ask you to do it? Or if it is something you can do by yourself, how would it glorify Him?

Don't take that to the extreme that something can't be good or God's will if it's in your power to do. But do realize that God sometimes calls you to "impossible" things because they are impossible without Him and He loves to come through for you.

Take heart, friends. God enjoys giving us the kingdom. Whatever He asks, do it, no matter how silly or impossible it seems. In the end, have faith that you will see a move of the Most High and that He will use you for His glory. Don't listen to the scoffers, but stand on Who your God is and what He is capable of. His team always wins.

After everything is over, then you can look around for those who said that you would never succeed because what you were doing had never been done. If you really want to find them, though, you may have to dig.

Scriptures for meditation:

Joshua 5:13 – 6:27
Psalm 18:31 – 42
Isaiah 55:10 – 11
Psalm 37:3 – 4
Hebrews 11

Make it real:

•   Ask the Lord to resurrect any dreams He placed in your heart you've allowed to die because of opposition or lack of faith. Repent where needed.

•   Re-read at least two of your favorite Bible stories. If you're not sure where to look I recommend the story of Gideon and the miracles of Moses at the Red Sea. Let the reality of these events remind you of God's faithfulness and His power to do the "impossible."

•   Ask Holy Spirit to reveal God's plans for the dreams He has given you. He may give you the full blueprint now, or He may reveal the next step. As you receive, walk it out in faith.

•   Command the words spoken against you because of your kingdom dreams to be condemned (Isaiah 54:17). Ask the Lord to heal any wounds in your heart from words spoken against you, especially words from family, friends, or people you trust.

•   Ask for new kingdom dreams. Write down anything the Lord shows you. Keep something handy to write on or talk into so that you can record anything God gives you. As the pieces come together, remember to be obedient and walk in faith.

Part Three: Born Into A War

Hundreds of thousands of people in this world have never known something we in America take for granted: peace. From the time they were born to the time they die, these poor souls witness the horrors and injustices of wars that began before they existed and will likely continue after they pass away.

In the spiritual realm, every human being has the same story.

When we were born, we joined the oldest and most vicious conflict that has ever taken place. It is the battle between good and evil, between the kingdom of heaven and the forces of hell. Many deny the war exists. Many realize the severity of it but lack the knowledge to effectively join it. Many have left the battle, forgetting that the enemy doesn't stop fighting just because a believer does

It is a scary truth, but it is truth. The war is real. Thank God He has won it and has empowered His sons and daughters to fight as victorious warriors.

15

Alamo Christianity

"Remember the Alamo!"

Even though the Battle of the Alamo took place over 150 years ago, it is still a fairly common thing in the state of Texas to hear references to that famous incident. We Texans see it as one of the many things we are quite proud of in our state's heritage, and if you spend much time in our fine state, odds are you'll hear the story.

The short version goes something like this: Texas had declared independence from Mexico. The Mexican army, led by General Antonio Lopez de Santa Anna, came and began reclaiming territory. The Alamo, previously a mission, was converted into a fort for a small garrison of Texan soldiers. As the Mexican army drew near, the Texans knew they could not withstand it, and they requested reinforcements. None arrived. On February 23, 1836, a thirteen day siege began in which around 200 Texans withstood approximately 1,500 Mexican soldiers.

During the course of the siege, the Mexican soldiers fired cannons into the mission for hours at a time, followed by surges of troops intended to overrun the damaged walls. Twice, the Mexican soldiers advanced, and twice the Texans repelled them. The third time, the Texas forces were overpowered, and the Alamo fell.

No Texans survived.

However, during the course of the siege, around 600 Mexican soldiers were killed or wounded, and the delay in taking the Alamo cost Santa Anna dearly in terms of his ability to finish his campaign. Due to the casualties suffered and the time it took Santa Anna to rejoin the main force in the main battle at San Jacinto, Texas General Sam Houston was able to prepare his troops against the coming onslaught. At San Jacinto, the Texan defenders dealt a crushing blow to Santa Anna's army, winning independence for what would become the Republic of Texas.

Propelling the Texan soldiers to victory was the news of the courageous stand made in San Antonio, expressed in a resounding cry: "Remember the Alamo!"

To this day, Texans treasure the story of the Alamo as a tale of bravery in the face of death, courage to stand for one's ideals regardless of the cost, and the "never say die" attitude so many of us respect. We love to point out that it was not a racially divided battle, but one in which people of several national backgrounds, including those of Mexican descent, stood against what they regarded as tyranny and corruption. And we celebrate the strength it took to continue fighting when it was obvious the battle would result in defeat. Most Texans will make a point of telling you that, though none of the defenders survived, they killed or wounded three of the enemy for every Texan that died.

Whether or not you are from Texas, I hope you understand why we Texans consider it such an inspiration.

But far too many Christians are living out their faith as if they're trapped in the Alamo. Many believers view this life as a siege situation in which the enemy blasts the tar out of our church walls while we fearfully wait out the attack. When the enemy comes in all-out assault, we do our best to repulse them, but deep down, many Christians honestly believe the battle we're in is one we will ultimately lose.

At least there is the consolation that after we lose, we get to go to heaven.

I used to see it that way, too. I had adopted the underdog

mentality, and I earnestly believed the best thing I could do was hold on until I died and went to be with Jesus or He came back to set things right. But that is an absolutely false worldview, probably created by the devil himself to keep saints from joining the battle wholeheartedly.

For one, Christians are not outnumbered! There are more of us than there are of our enemy. Think about the fall of Lucifer and those dumbbell angels who followed him. One-third of them fell. That means two-thirds of them are still with us. Our side more than doubles the enemy's side.

Secondly, as Scripture repeatedly points out, saints of God are mightier than the devil's agents as long as we're operating under the anointing of Holy Spirit. We are seated in heavenly places, above the principalities and powers. If we want to see demons, we look down, not up. That is the spiritual reality, and therefore, that is the only reality. Seeing the battle as a losing proposition is the illusion.

The same power that spoke everything into being dwells inside us. The same Man who overcame death, sin, and the dumb devil also promised He would always be with us. The same God who is omnipotent, omniscient, and omni-good (yeah I know, not a word) calls Himself my Dad and literally can't wait for me to ask Him to kick my enemy's sorry behind. And remember what Jesus said about those who believe in Him? He promised that we would heal the sick, cast out demons, cleanse lepers, and raise the dead.

Jesus healed more people than can be written about in four gospels in the Bible. He performed miracles, spoke blessings, defeated demons, overcame death, and went about doing good. He took twelve seemingly random dudes and used them to transform the earth. And, according to Jesus Himself, we get to do greater things than these!

So think about this. I mean it: really think about it. How many demons can one saint cast out? How much love can one man of God disperse in his lifetime? How many people could one person raise from the dead? How many wounds, injuries, and diseases can one woman of faith heal? How many lives can change simply because one person not only preached the gospel of Christ, but actually lived it out?

Let's make it real. My friends Guy and Caroline have defeated dozens, if not hundreds of demons in their lifetimes, and they're not even teenagers yet. I know of ministries that have documented hundreds of dead people brought back to life in the name of Jesus. I can point to generations of people and their families who walk lovingly with the Lord because of one faithful woman who stood for, on, and with king Jesus as He used her to transform lives. I know a guy who chases people down in the supermarket and heals them on a daily basis, while another man heals people simply by praying for them over the phone.

And these are just some of the ones I know about. I know there are more that I've never heard of. The point is that it's real! It's happening right now, and if they can do it, so can we!

Friends, we are not Alamo Christians. We are definitely under attack, but as big and strong as our enemies are, our ally, God Almighty, is greater still. Yes, we are in a war, but a pastor I used to know described it like this, "I've read the Book. We win!" We're not waiting around for the defeat; we're looking forward to the final victory and doing our part in bringing it about.

One of the most famous stories from the Alamo happened on March 3, 1836, just a few days before the Alamo was overtaken. William Barrett Travis, the commander of the remaining Texas forces, surmised that he would not emerge from the battle victorious. In the last letter he ever composed, Travis said he would never surrender. For him, the choice was victory or death. He called his soldiers together and plainly told them they would die if they stayed to fight. Then, he took his sword and drew a line in the dirt. He said all were welcome to leave if they wished, but he ordered all who would stay and fight to cross over the line. All but one man chose to stay. They sacrificed their lives for their ideals and earned their place in history. Their sacrifice led to the eventual victory.

Jesus has done the same thing, only with different choices.

He has taken His sword and drawn the line. He doesn't force anyone to come to His side, but the choice is clear: cross the line and join Him, or go. Those who leave will have their just reward in eternity. Those who fight in the army of the Lamb will find their place in the kingdom of heaven. This is not a new saying. "Choose you this day whom you will serve." Victory or death.

As for me and my house, we will serve the Lord of the victorious.

Scriptures for meditation:

Psalm 18, which sums up the end of the battle.
Revelation 19:17-21

Make it Real:

•   Change your thinking about the spiritual war. If you see yourself as being on the losing side, renounce that viewpoint right now.
•   Ask Holy Spirit to reveal the truth to you. Jesus is always victorious. Claim 2 Corinthians 2:14 for yourself. God always leads us in triumph.
•   Numbers do not matter. With God, the odds are always on your side.

16

Love Grenades

If I were in the army, I would want to be the guy with all the grenades. I know that's not how they do things, I'm just saying. I like grenades because they are not finesse weapons. If you get a grenade anywhere near the bad guys, the bad guys go boom. It doesn't take much skill to learn to use a grenade, either. Pull the pin, throw it in the general direction of the enemy you want to take out, and pow! No more enemy.

It's my kind of weapon!

Now what if I were to tell you that you are a walking, talking grenade in the hands of the Holy Spirit? Cool, right?

Every single believer has been hand crafted by God Himself to accomplish works which He already has planned for us. The result of these works is twofold. First, it brings God pleasure and glorifies Him. Second, it blows up the dominion of the devil and makes him look stupid. That's exactly why Satan has worked so hard to convince the saints of God that they really don't have anything to offer the kingdom of heaven.

You probably know someone who really doesn't think much of himself. He has some amazing qualities that encourage you in some way, yet he can point to fifteen people who have that quality more than he does. Or perhaps you know a woman who is extremely gifted in several areas, but she belittles them and claims they are not as important as things other people do.

The devil has worked extremely hard to convince believers that the only things that matter to God take place inside the church walls or are directly tied to some kind of ministry. Basically, he lies to us saying, "If you're not a pastor, evangelist, or missionary, you really don't matter."

If you're anything like me, you grew tired long ago with the idea that all good and worthy pursuits are in some way connected to church. While it is true that all good and worthy pursuits will in some way advance the kingdom of heaven or bring God pleasure, it is also true that there are not enough pastor positions out there for all of us. Plus, if we were all pastors, who would we pastor? And besides that, not everyone is called to an "official" position of ministry.

Yet so many Christians sit around in discouragement because the things they truly love to do have little or nothing to do with "church."

For example, I love to fish. I don't feel guilty when I spend a day fishing instead of reading my Bible. How does that advance the kingdom? I have no idea other than that I suspect it gives God great pleasure when I enjoy the planet He created to share with me. Sure I pray when I'm out there by myself. Sure I often use that time to enjoy fellowship with other believers, also known as talking with my buddies, but mostly I just enjoy attempting to catch fish. Funny as this may sound, I really used to wonder if God was going to make me stop fishing because it wasn't "holy."

A friend of mine recently shared how she actually felt guilty for having a strong desire to bake a cake one afternoon. Her reasoning was something like this: "Well I could have been studying the Bible for all that time it took me. And this cake is something I really don't need. Plus, I know of people out there right now witnessing on the streets, so it must really not be godly for me to be baking a cake instead of doing those other things."

I'm sure you know someone who has sounded like that

at times. The reason this kind of thinking occurs is that we feel guilty for not being "spiritual" enough. For example, it's okay for someone to write Christian songs all day or spend hours reading a Bible study book, but it's not okay to sew just because you enjoy sewing.

That's the mindset a lot of Christians have, but that's not God's mindset. God is absolutely fine with me spending a day fishing. He's also okay with my friend baking a cake or with you spending an afternoon sewing. After all, He's the One Who made us with those desires.

Think about what the Bible is saying when it tells us that the God of the universe fashioned us with His own hands. Everything else snapped into being by His word, but He lovingly formed us out of the clay. One Psalm describes God gently knitting us together piece by piece in our mothers' wombs. He didn't say, "Let there be people!" He carefully, individually formed each of us exactly the way He wanted us to be. Before I was born, He knew what I would look like. He knew I would like chocolate and despise beets. He knew corny jokes would make me laugh, and He knew how much I would like to fish.

He knew because that's how He made me.

May I suggest that my fishing gives God pleasure because I'm doing something He created for me to enjoy? Would it be too much to believe that God likes it when someone doodles just because that doodling was His idea?

Now, don't take this as permission to just do whatever you want whenever you want to do it. If God is asking me to go on a street outreach and I choose to go fishing instead, I have rebelled against Him. I'm not suggesting that you replace obedience to God with your personal desires. I am suggesting that there may be a larger purpose for the things you simply love to do.

See, I don't believe in insignificant people or insignificant parts of people. If God took the time to give me a trait, it must be important.

Imagine God walked up to you one day and handed you a penny. You wouldn't take it, and then later toss it away because it was just a penny. That penny was a gift from God, and you'd treasure it the rest of your life. You'd even tell stories about the time God gave you a penny, and odds are, your stories would encourage and uplift the people you told.

Yet, we somehow look at certain parts of ourselves or our personality and deem them insignificant. We haven't learned to treasure ourselves.

Beloved, God does treasure every part of us He created. That's why He works so hard to deliver us from the wounds, perversions, and flat-out demonic invasions on His original idea. He wants us to be who He created us to be.

When God made everything, He knew there would be a special place in the kingdom that only you could fill. He designed it that way on purpose. Without you, the kingdom is incomplete. That means there are no insignificant people in the kingdom. We're all important, and we all need each other! Furthermore, just because you may not have been called to walk in as much of the spotlight as someone else, that doesn't mean your part is any less essential.

I thank God there are men and women like Bill Johnson, Patricia King, and Todd Bentley out there doing what they're doing. I admire them and many more like them, but as great as they are, even they can't get around to everybody. They're not supposed to. God never intended to throw the burden of rocking the world with the gospel upon a select few. It's everybody's job, and it's supposed to be everybody's joy.

Yes, you read that right. It's supposed to be a joy. Why do you think God made all of us just a little weird? Why did He plant that little desire in Bob, but not in Jerry? Why does Mae like to cook, while Juanita absolutely loves giving away presents? Because that's God's sneaky way of giving us all grenades!

He made us so that together we would grow up into the perfect body of Jesus Christ. As a whole, we lack nothing, but we are altogether equipped and perfect to subdue the earth to the dominion of king Jesus. Individually, we seem like a hodgepodge group of weirdos, but from God's point of view, we form the body of a mighty warrior as every part does its job. To make sure we all do our part, He made things fun for us!

So what is it that you really love to do? If you love to make lemonade and sit around with friends, do it. Use that opportunity to be encouraged or to hand out encouragement. Take the chance you have to grow together. Or just realize that, even if no "spiritual" things take place, people need to know that someone cares enough to make lemonade and offer it to them. Jesus called that love, and love is the most spiritual thing there is.

Give gifts, go fishing, climb mountains, write poetry, or do whatever it is that you love to do, and do it realizing that in each of those things, there are opportunities for you to share the love of Jesus. Sometimes, you're advancing the kingdom simply because you showed up and the kingdom happens to be inside you.

Also, realize that those things that really light up your heart may be a physical picture of what you are in the spirit. My love of fishing is mirrored by my passion for evangelism. Fishing for men is a lot like fishing for fish, but even more fun because of the miracles.

So what burns in your heart? Do you like to repair things? If so, you may also notice you have a knack for mending broken hearts or offering just the right encouragement at just the right time. I'd imagine there's at least one person who loves it when you come because you build their fragile heart up the same way you build up those broken objects. You may not even have to say anything; they just take strength from your presence.

Do you bake? If so, I bet you also are pretty good at taking a little revelation from here, a word you heard there, tucking them away for a time, and eventually coming up with a greater and more delicious spiritual truth than what you had when you started. Sometimes it takes the heat of testing for all this to happen, but you produce sweetness in the end.

It may not be the case in every situation, but many times we mirror our spiritual purposes in the day-to-day activities we perform. Whatever yours is, I'm sure you will notice it if you pay attention. Or you could just ask Holy Spirit to reveal it. Either way, realize that you have a special place in the kingdom, which only your personality or talents can fill.

When the people of God put their talents, desires, and qualities to work, He gets glorified and Satan gets defeated. That glass of lemonade you shared was a spiritual grenade lobbed at enemy troops. It wasn't hard for you, but it sure was effective. That makes it even more fun!

Think of the possibilities here. Someone loves to tell jokes. One of their jokes brightens the day of a kid suffering with depression. Blam-o! The door opens up for Jesus to minister joy and break the hold of heaviness. Another person loves to garden. The guy walking up the street sees the garden and for one second ponders the glory of God's creation. Pow! Take that devil! What if someone who loved to hunt took a fatherless kid hunting for a weekend and simply showed him some love? What if an animal lover volunteered to walk an elderly neighbor's dogs once or twice a week? What if an artist did face painting for kids and gave the proceeds to charity?

Oh my goodness! Now we're venturing off into overt gestures of love and service. That's dangerous, people. All it really comes down to is that you have a bunch of things that you truly enjoy doing, and every single one of them can and does advance the kingdom of heaven. Not to mention that every believer can prophesy, cast out demons, heal the sick, give, and love freely. Maybe that special hobby of yours is meant to open up doors for you to do those very things.

And every time we do those things, part of hell gets blown up. I don't know about you, but that sure sounds like fun to me.

Scriptures for meditation:

Ephesians 3:10
Romans 13:8-14
1 Timothy 4:14
1 Peter 4:7-11
Romans 12

Make it real:

• Think of the things you truly love to do. Ask Holy Spirit to show you how those things advance the kingdom. Then put them to use. Enjoy your grenades.

• Never miss a chance to bless someone, or to tell them how much they mean to you. Simple acts are often the most powerful. Ask Holy Spirit who he wants to bless, and within the next three days, use your talents, gifts, and abilities to bless them in some way. Pray for that person in the meantime and watch what God does.

• Daily living is warfare in itself. Love is the most powerful weapon you have, and you can have as much as you want. Let love come through your everyday activity, and see what a difference it makes in the lives of the people around you. You're advancing heaven when you love freely.

• "Overcome evil with good." If you need motivation to get out there and do good, remember that Jesus said, "Inasmuch as you did it to one of the least of these My brethren, you did it to Me." Picture Jesus, and do it as if it were really Him. That's how He will take it, whether you do anything or not. What would you be willing to do to see Jesus smile?

17

Stir

Jesus is serious. He's not messing around because He cannot afford to, and neither can His saints. The time is drawing short, the battle intensifies, and the time has come for the warriors of the kingdom to rise up, carry the banner of Christ, and assume our positions in the ranks of heaven's army. But too many of us are asleep.

I don't know how to put this mildly, so I'm just going to be blunt. If you can read this and not be stirred, you need to ask the Lord to awaken you to the truth of your existence and the urgency of your purpose.

I give no glory to the enemy, nor do I hope to create fear for anyone who reads. Take this as a wakeup call to every man, woman, and child who bears the name of Jesus.

To really get ahold of what I'm talking about, let me take you back to right after the fall. Lucifer, once one of the most beautiful of all the angels in heaven, had lost the battle against Michael and the host. The angels who followed Lucifer were banished from the glory, sentenced to an eternity of separation from the Presence of God Almighty. Lucifer, corrupted and growing more so all the time, transformed into Satan the Accuser, while his army degenerated into the hosts of darkness.

If you have ever wondered what utter defeat looks like, this was it.

Not only did Satan realize his defeat, but he also knew there was no way he could ever oppose God Almighty, whose servants had cast him into outer darkness. And to add insult to injury, God had taken His glory and given it to mere humans. Thus was born the burning hatred of our enemy.

Satan's vehement hatred of mankind knew no limit. It burned hotter than a volcano and erupted violently and frequently. And this enemy, bursting with unquenchable wrath, set in motion his plan to rob mankind of every blessing God intended for them.

He deceived Eve to get to Adam, and when Adam submitted to Satan's will rather than God's, the accuser gained free access to this world. The enemy unleashed all his hosts, all his powers, and all his ruling princes to wreak havoc on the world. Their job description was simple: kill, steal, and destroy.

Let us not deceive ourselves. These are no ordinary enemies sent against us. They are thousands of years old, and though they stupidly rebelled against God, they are still clever and very skilled at hiding. They sow seeds of discord like a farmers sows cotton seeds. They weave lies ceaselessly and without remorse. They breed bitterness, stir selfishness, awaken anger, and scheme relentlessly against humans.

They know the time is short until Jesus returns, and their sole mission between now and then is to rend God's heart by destroying as many of those created in His image as they possibly can. They are strong, they are smart, and they are on a mission fueled by the surpassingly hot fire of their fallen master.

They have no sense of honor. They have no shame. They have no boundaries, no morals, and no mercy. They are just has happy to destroy infants as they are to overcome the elderly. They rape women, shame men, and confuse children. They lay traps everywhere. They lure, deceive, tempt, lie, and attack with no quarter and no intent of taking prisoners, save for those they intend to use or possess.

These enemies crush ministries. They divide churches with argument and bitterness. They separate and destroy families. They pervert true intimacy. They accuse the Father to the children, and the children to the Father. They have even worked tirelessly to smear the meaning of "father," "mother," and "family." They know that if these vital relationships can be perverted in people's minds, then the sons and daughters of the kingdom will struggle to understand the love of God.

They work tirelessly to shut off people from God's compassion. They never stop.

They are always stealing, always killing, and always seeking to destroy the lives of humans. That, my brothers and sisters, is our enemy.

And let's take a minute to make this personal. These enemies I'm talking about, these spiritual hosts of wickedness, they're after you. They'll get you any way they can, and they're not picky. They never come at you when you're feeling strong, but they sure will kick you when you're down. They sneak up on you when you're not looking. They wait patiently until you're tired or weakened, then they spring their traps.

But they're not just after you. They are after your mother and your father. They're after your relationships. They want to ruin your friendships. They want to drive walls between you and the people you care about most. They want distrust and perversion to replace openness and intimacy.

They're after your marriage. They laugh when you give into anger, or when you mistrust your spouse. They rejoice when you feel too tired to pursue the one you love. They revel in rejection, and they dance on depression. They love it when you feel lonely in your own house. They would like nothing more than for you and your spouse to settle for anything less than the fullness God intended for your marriage because if you receive the fullness of marriage, you have revelation of one of God's best pictures of your relationship with Him.

Are you angry yet?

They're after your children, too. They don't care if your

child isn't old enough to walk yet, or if she's a teenager. Anything they can do to help you hurt your kids, they consider the highest joy. They love helping you wound your kids with your words. They love keeping you too busy to keep your promises. And all those things they're doing to you, they're also doing to your kids.

Does this make you want to fight?

Good.

Maybe now you see why Jesus is stirring the hearts of the saints to rise up and do battle. Maybe now you see why "church" was never intended to be a passive participation in a religious service, but an active reliance on and submission to Holy Spirit as He moves on the earth. Maybe now you understand why it's important that we warn every single person we know that as humans, we were born into a war that is older than our race and more intense than any conflict that has ever occurred on our planet. It's real, it's happening right now, and it's not going to go away because we ignore it.

Friends, one of the best strategies Satan has used to keep believers from joining Holy Spirit in this struggle is the lie that all there is for us is to get saved, read the Bible, try to live a decent life, and wait around to die so we can go be with Jesus. All of that is good, but that's not all there is!

God's original plan was for humans to have dominion on the earth and spread His kingdom, and He hasn't changed His mind! Jesus died to restore us to our original mission given in the Garden. We don't wait on the kingdom to come; we are vessels through which the kingdom comes right now!

The other major strategy Satan uses is convincing saints that we are no match for him. This is a half-truth, which makes it a full lie. Satan and all his hosts were put to an open shame on the cross. Holy Spirit is more than a match for the devil, and the devil knows it. Holy Spirit lives in the saints, and He is the one whose power we exert against the messengers of hell. The Word of God by which all things were created is still alive and still just as powerful as it ever was! And the Lord has chosen to put that word in the mouths of those who serve Him.

No my friends, our weapons are not weak, but mighty in God for pulling down strongholds, casting down arguments, and utterly defeating anything that opposes the knowledge of God.

It is a matter of obedience. We have our marching orders from Jesus. We are to go and make disciples. We are to heal the sick, cleanse the lepers, and cast out demons. We are to use the gifts Holy Spirit has given us to bring the kingdom of heaven to earth and to carry out God's will.

Please realize that you are in the war whether you wanted to be or not. If you belong to Jesus, you have already proclaimed that your life is His, so you have agreed to stand with Him. On behalf of your friends, your family, and the rest of mankind, stir yourself up. Let your heart blaze with passion. Let your spirit soar. Let Holy Spirit show you your place in the lines, and take up your sword!

The time for passive Christianity has passed. In fact, it has never existed. Jesus demonstrated what passion for the Father looked like, so let us follow his example in love and loyalty. Let us take the Word of God seriously. Let us worship with all our hearts and all our strength. Let us become obedient to the point of death. Let us live under the power of Holy Spirit.

Let us fight!

Scriptures for meditation:

Ephesians 6:10-13
1 Peter 5:6-11
Luke 22:31-32
1 Timothy 4:1-4
Revelation 12:7-12, 17

Make it real:

•   I cannot stress enough the importance of spiritual warfare. The enemy is after you, whether you are fighting him or not. Your prayers, your worship, your declaration of the Word of God, and all the other weapons you have been given must not lie dormant! Ask Holy Spirit to show you the weapons of your warfare. Ask Him every day to show you where to fight and how. He always leads you in triumph.
•   If you have believed you cannot win the battles in your life, repent immediately. You have believed the enemy's lies. Jesus never fails. Ask God's forgiveness for giving heed to lies. He will forgive you, and He will teach your hands to make war. Greater is He who is in you than he who is in the world.
•   If you don't feel you know enough about spiritual warfare to engage in it effectively, equip yourself! Ask Holy Spirit to teach you to be a warrior for Jesus. Get resources if you need them to help you grow in this area. A couple books I highly recommend are Lauren Caldwell's There's No Junior Holy Spirit and Henry Malone's Shadow Boxing. These two books teach principles of spiritual warfare effectively and in a way that is easy to understand and put to immediate use. You may be encouraged to know that many people have written about spiritual warfare. However, I do recommend that you seek the guidance of Holy Spirit in this area. He will show you where to find what you need to win your battle.

18

Might

I have to be honest: I get really aggravated sometimes when I look at the way the church portrays our Savior. Seriously, look at the stained glass images in our sanctuaries. Observe carefully the way our books or movies characterize the Son of God.

In our pictures or stained glass representations, Jesus often looks very much the part of the suffering servant, eyes upturned miserably toward heaven, seemingly resigned to the terrible life He took upon himself. The expression on His face seems to say, "What have I gotten myself into?" The crucifix often shows a scrawny Jesus dangling helplessly from the cross with a pathetic countenance that begs for pity.

In movies, Jesus stoically walks from one place to the next, vaguely and morosely relaying the truths of the kingdom to a mystified rabble of followers. He slowly and without passion lays hands on the sick and, in a voice that sounds like someone just waking up, says lamely, "Be healed." And, boredom of boredoms, they are. Whoop-tee-doo. On He goes to his next chore. I watch and can't help wondering, "Did Jesus ever smile?" Surely He wasn't a cardboard man who never showed any feeling. Yet, that is exactly how He appears in a great number of Christian movies.

We give honor to that person in the picture because we know who He is supposed to be, but what if you met that man in real life, and He acted the way He is shown?

You'd probably think He was puny and weird.

Praise God that He can use even these attempts at representing Jesus to reach hearts and save souls, but give me a break, people! If a faulty picture of my Lord can inspire people, I would be thrilled to see what would happen if they saw the real thing.

Of course I realize Jesus wasn't the picture of strength and glory when He hung on the cross. That was His darkest hour, and I'm sure (as Scripture describes) He looked more like a beaten piece of meat than the king of heaven. I know that He wept uncontrollably and was disturbed to the point of sweating blood in Gethsemane. But compared to the entirety of His life, and held next to the grandeur of His eternal reign, these moments of Jesus' existence are less than blinks.

We do not worship a puny Savior! Quite the opposite is true: we worship the mightiest warrior and the greatest lover who has ever existed.

Consider what Jesus left behind to come here in the first place. He had it all, literally. Yet He left it all to come get me! Me! That tells me He was either crazy or desperately in love, and I know He was not crazy. That only leaves one way to look at it.

Have you ever seen someone completely lovesick? They do not in any way resemble cardboard. I imagine Jesus lost in rapturous thought, smiling mischievously as He plans the next tryst with His beloved. I can almost hear His quiet giggles as His overflowing heart rushes to the surface. Scripture records Jesus's eyes as flames of fire, reflecting His intense desire for His bride. Jesus has always lived from His heart of unabated passion.

When He walked this earth in the form of a man, Jesus was full of a Creator's joy as He experienced firsthand the beauty of His creation. Every song He heard, every sound of cattle, every rainstorm, and every child's laugh filled Him with unimaginable joy. When He touched a person or listened to a joke, He did not do it without emotion. When something went wrong, He did not simply go on about his business, or fix it as if it were of no consequence. I imagine He laughed as heartily and cried as bitterly as anyone I've ever met.

But He's not merely a sensitive romantic; He's a man's man. Consider that Jesus grew up as a carpenter in a time with no power tools. He knew hard labor, and I would bet my car that He was built like a wrestler. I'm sure He had an iron grip when He wanted to, and I would definitely not arm wrestle the Man! After all, He once drove gaggle of moneylenders out of the temple single-handedly. I have a hard time imagining a puny little dude running in and striking terror into the heart of these evil-minded men. Yet they fled before the real Jesus.

And you know He messed with His disciples. "Hey Peter, go throw your hook in the lake and bring back the gold coin from the fish's mouth." Can you see Peter scratching his head and mumbling as he walked off to go fishing? And John told us plainly Jesus did so many things the earth could not contain them. I can't help but wonder if there is a volume somewhere of Jesus' pranks.

Jesus is God the Son, author of life, creator of joy, inventor of passion. Yet, the enemy has so schemed and lied to us about Him that many believers see Jesus as this unemotional weakling. Those devils know they have to stop people from seeing the truth about Jesus because if people understand who He is and who they are in Him, the devils will spend the rest of their existence getting their butts kicked.

First off, Jesus didn't argue with Father God about coming to the earth. He wasn't in heaven pleading with Dad not to send Him. Quite the opposite is true: He was waiting eagerly for the appointed time to come get His bride. As I have said, Jesus was desperately in love, and there is no stopping a man in love, let alone the Son of Man in love.

That He would leave heaven because of us is the greatest act of love ever committed, and it took more strength of character than any other person has.

Besides that, Jesus is the mightiest warrior the world has ever known.

The Bible says that when Jesus died on the cross, He disarmed the principalities and powers. Basically, He defeated every devil there is, even the most fearsome, and took away their powers. "Disarmed" (Colossians 2:15) means they are no longer armed. That doesn't mean they can't mimic spiritual weaponry and attack. It does mean that the weapons of the enemy shall no longer prosper against us, that they have lost their power over us, and that they are beaten. Can I get a boo-yeah?!

That's how strong Jesus was. He went to the cross and died as a sacrifice, but He rose as a victorious king. Not even death could stop this warrior in love.

On top of that, Jesus commands an army of angels, and these are not the sweet, placid, gift-shop angels. These are the real deal. Whenever someone in the Bible encountered one of these guys, the typical response was to fall flat on one's face and tremble. That tells us they can be terrifying to behold, yet none of them would allow people to grovel before them. They always said, "Don't worship me; worship God." You see, these angels knew they served a king even greater than they were, and even these majestic and terrible beings wouldn't dare take His glory.

To put that in perspective, consider that the Bible records a time when one single angel slew 185,000 men in one night. That's one bad mamma-jamma. However, if the mighty angel who performed that amazing feat were in a room and Jesus walked in, that angel would fall on its face in holy dread.

An angel did rebel against God once, and he and those who followed him will reap their eternal reward soon enough. The amazing thing is that Satan and the angels who fell with him never even got to face off against Jesus. Michael and the angelic host threw Satan down from heaven, and Michael himself bows before Jesus.

What does that tell you about Jesus?

Our king not only destroyed all the weapons of our enemy,

He also commands an army of dedicated and incredibly powerful warriors who exist for the sole purpose of carrying out His word. That's how mighty our king is, and we haven't even talked about the power of Jesus' name.

You can tell how powerful someone is by what happens when you mention their name. Even in human terms, when someone says, "The boss wants all those boxes moved up that flight of stairs," something happens. The task may be difficult and the boss may not even be present, but the workers still carry it out because the boss's name was mentioned. They know there are consequences for disobeying and potential rewards for obeying. The more power, or might, a person has, the more will happen at the mention of their name.

At the mention of the name of Jesus, blind eyes open, bones re-grow, and deaf ears hear. Sickness flees. The dead return to life. Cancer disappears. Souls are restored and even saved. Mere humans covered in the tarnish of sin may step into the very presence of the Most High God, and not only are they not destroyed, they actually become clean in His sight, and they even receive His eternal and unfailing blessing. By the authority of the name of Jesus, demons are cast out. Jesus is so powerful that even the minions of hell obey when saints of God use His name. At the name of Jesus, the supposedly mighty enemy is utterly defeated.

That is might.

So, on the one hand, we believers have very strong enemies who constantly attempt to steal from us, kill us, or destroy any part of our lives they can. They're bigger than we are, older than we are, stronger than we are by ourselves, and they've got nothing else to do but mess things up for us. But on the other hand, we have our beautiful King Jesus, who is not a weakling, but a mighty warrior who has already defeated the enemy and continues to defeat them every minute of every day.

The church must break out of the deceptive way of thinking that the darkness is big and the kingdom is little. We serve the God of might, the God of victory, and the God of all power. And it is absolutely okay for believers to be powerful. God never intended for us to just get by. He promised life more abundantly, and He equipped us with the power to live it out! We must realize that the power is His, not ours, and we must give Him all the glory for it. But the fact remains: saints are vessels meant to carry and release the power of the kingdom of heaven. Jesus died to restore to us what God intended us to have all along: the power to kick devil butt and spread the kingdom to all the earth.

Brothers and sisters, our side is the winning team. Our side is the big side. The enemy is and always will be the underdog to Jesus and His might.

And the only way we can get this revelation ingrained in our spirit is to know Jesus. The more we know Him, the more we love Him. The more we love him, the more we obey Him. The more we obey Him, the more we encounter His mighty power as it comes on us, to us, and through us. And the more we encounter Him, the more we love Him.

That love is what defeats the enemy every time. As you'll see in the next chapter, love makes you dangerous.

Scriptures for meditation:
Revelation 1:9-20
Colossians 2:13-15
2 Chronicles 32:20-22
Isaiah 37:31-38
Psalm 24:8
Isaiah 42:13
Ephesians 1:18-23

Make it real:
•   If you've given the enemy glory by believing he is mightier than Jesus, look at the Scriptures above and let them invade your heart. Repent and renounce the lie that the enemy is mighty. Make the confession that Jesus is Lord over ALL! Nothing is mightier than He.

•   Ask for revelation of the Spirit of Might, and how Holy Spirit can unleash His mighty power in your life. He will.

•   Obedience is key. If you want to see God's power come on you, to you, and through you, you must obey Him. It's like He's given you a nuclear bomb in the spirit, but you must allow Him to instruct you on how to use it. He will teach you, but you must obey when you hear Him. As always, do not allow condemnation for your mistakes to drag you down. Repent, receive forgiveness, and keep pursuing obedience to God. Hint: it all comes from loving Him.

•   If you find yourself discouraged by bad news, world events, or the simple realization that this world is dark, change your focus. Remember that light always overcomes darkness. Remember that Jesus is mighty enough to change all of it, and that you are one of His favorite ways to do so. God's not scared or worried. His instruction is simple: Shine your light! Overcome evil with good!

19

Unstoppable

What compels people to give their lives for a cause? Dying in the name of another person, an ideal, or a country shows the kind of determination mere intellectual assent could never arouse, nor could the necessity of duty. There has to be something more than just a conscious decision at work in people who willingly die for their beliefs.

That something is love.

For some, the love of country propels them to the front of the battle. They leave behind wives, children, and native lands to fight for a country they believe is worth giving their lives. Their blood testifies of loyalty and patriotism. That willingly given blood is the finest measure of a country's greatness.

Others see wrongs that must be defeated at all costs. These people speak out against the majority, against the norm, and against the injustices that simply cannot be tolerated. They surrender their dignity and status in favor of a righteous cause. Their legacies cry out to successive generations to remember and to act.

Still others discover such love for a particular person that they simply refuse to surrender. No matter the cost, these lovers willingly forfeit their safety, their comfort, and even their body organs to save the ones they love. They will fight even when outnumbered. They will endure excruciating pain. If it costs them their lives, they will not flinch, but they will step forward with the sure steps of heroic self-sacrifice and say, "Here I am."

Love is crazy.

At least, that's the way it looks to someone who has never experienced the depths of that love, either as recipient or as giver. Love insists that it has won, even when all signs point to the contrary. It never backs down. Love trumps suffering, casts down selfishness, spurns bribes, and detests even the suggestion that it should settle for than anything less than absolute fullness. And if you're not under the influence of love, the people who are look like lunatics.

Jesus' undiluted love made the Pharisees think He was a madman. He walked right into their temples and taught with power and authority, demonstrating at every turn that the kingdom of heaven was at hand. They threatened His life, yet He continued on His way. They tried to trick Him with arguments and reason, but He refuted them with higher Truth. They tried to flatter Him, to get Him to just shut up, to shut Him down, yet He continued to send out the invitation to His wedding to those who had ears to hear.

It must have been terrible for the Pharisees to realize they could do absolutely nothing to stop this seemingly insane carpenter from Nazareth. Everything they tried only seemed to stir Jesus' passion, and at every turn His love made their religion seem foolish. Even worse for the religious elite, people were starting to believe in Him.

That's a beautiful side effect of love. Shameless, selfless love inspires trust, and trust holds hands with faith. School teachers repeat the saying, "Nobody cares what you know until they know you care." Love proves that it cares by offering itself freely. Love breaks through and reaches people when reason and logic have miserably failed.

Throughout His life, Jesus proclaimed to the people, "I love you enough to give Myself to you." Later, He showed us all He loved us enough to give Himself for us.

Jesus wrote us a love letter in His own blood, which makes

it both terrible and precious. Of all the lovers in history, Jesus of Nazareth is the only one to go as deep and as far for love as He did. If you add up what He left behind in heaven, the servant nature He took up while on earth, and what He endured in the name of love during His final passion, that sum eclipses any other measure of love. Not even hell itself could stop the love of Jesus Christ.

God proves His immeasurable love for us because He did all that while we were still His avowed enemies. Our Father's love changed the world forever, and it continues to change the world for His purposes. This love is greater than a cause, greater than romance, and greater than the earth itself. It is greater than anything hell can throw at us.

That is the degree of love with which our Father has filled His children. It is the length and width and height and depth of a love beyond anything this world can even comprehend. Yet, God has given His beloved the invitation to experience it, swim in it, and be swept away by it.

That's where the victory begins for believers. Every single Christian must encounter the raging torrent of love pouring from the Father's heart. We must all come to know how much Daddy loves us, how much our Bridegroom adores us, how much the great Spirit of Truth burns for us. We must get staggering drunk in God's presence. We must laugh until it hurts and weep from the purest joy and sweetest brokenness we have ever known. Then we must allow Him to draw us deeper, further, and higher than ever before.

The key to winning the spiritual war all of us were born into is to immerse ourselves in love, to let it in, let it come to us, and let it come through us. When we know how much God loves us, we are empowered to love others. When we love others more than ourselves, we live the life God intended for us, and hell loses.

The victory comes in two ways. First, love for God works itself out through obedience. Someone enamored with the Father doesn't care how crazy the request seems. She cares more about what God says than what nature, people, or society has to offer on the subject. "Walk on water? Sure, Dad, I'll do that for you."

In Gethsemane, knowing the immense affliction that He was about to suffer, Jesus still loved His Daddy and His bride enough to obey. It wasn't a question for Him. He was in love with God, and that mattered the most. Plus, He knew what prize awaited Him.

What about us? What would we accomplish if we let God ravish our hearts to the point where we seriously didn't care whether we lived or died, so long as we glorified God? Religion would lose its stranglehold on believers if they had no regard for the traditions of men. Fear of suffering or rejection would go the way of the Dodo as believers realized how ridiculous fear is in the face of love. It would be impossible to shut someone down whose motto was, "For me, to live is Christ, and to die is gain!" Just ask those poor folks who tried to stop Paul from preaching the gospel.

They once stoned Paul to "death" for preaching Jesus. They drug his seemingly lifeless body outside the city and left him there. Then, by the miraculous power of Holy Spirit, Paul hopped up and went right back into the city to preach some more. What could you possibly do to stop someone like that?

The other way love wins is that it shows up, regardless of the circumstances. There is no place love fears to tread and no person love despises to touch. Love humbles itself, caring more about saving the person in front of it than about reputations, rumors, or religious boundaries. From the smallest acts of kindness to the day-in-day-out relationship building of true ministry, love removes barriers and pierces to the heart.

Stories abound about hard-hearted people who earnestly believed all they deserved was to suffer and die until someone cared about them enough to show them love. Reasons melt away in the passion of genuine love. Wounds knit themselves back together in the balm of tenderness. Bitter grimaces can easily turn to delighted grins with something as simple as a thoughtful gift. Most importantly, when believers show the world love, they open the door for the author of love to come. We raise the banner that says, "I love you enough to be here for you." Then, when they ask why, we get the honor of telling them Who has sent us to invite them to the feast.

All of these things happen by the love of our Father.

The love of God transforms ordinary believers into men and women of valor. Genuine love for the Lord and genuine love for people transform normally tame and civil individuals into power outlets unleashing the fury of heaven in the darkness of the world. It makes people unafraid of consequences. Lovers stare physical harm right in the eye without blinking. A Christian in love has no regard even for death itself.

Love makes hell look tiny.

God's purposes for us may be so deep and complex that we spend our entire lives searching them out, yet one overarching goal remains: God wants to transform us into the image of His Son so we can change the world with His love. He wants us to be sold out madmen preaching the gospel unashamedly before kings. He wants us to be the compassionate body of Christ ministering to the beaten down and broken in the streets. He wants us to function like a war machine crushing the ranks of our enemies like ants as worship and the unity of the Spirit drive us onward.

Love makes the sons and daughters of God unstoppable, just like Jesus.

Our Lord is raising up an army of soldiers who love Him more than anything else. He's teaching them to love because love is the greatest weapon in the arsenal of heaven. Love defeats fear, hate, and all the other tricks and schemes of the devil. If you want to see the victory of Jesus in every area of your life, and if you truly want to be effective in His service, the instructions are simple.

1. Lie down.
2. Die to self.
3. Fall in love.
4. Repeat often.

Love never fails; Jesus always wins.

Scriptures for meditation:

Romans 5:8-10
Philippians 1:19-21; 29
1 John 2:12-14
1 John 3, which shows why love is so important
1 John 4:17
1 John 5:1-5

Make it real:

All the mighty Christians I know have this in common: every day they ask God to reveal His great love for them. Then they wait until they see, feel, or perceive that love. Even Jesus commanded His disciples that they should wait until they had been endued with power from on high before they preached to all the world (Luke 24: 49). You must encounter God's love on a daily basis. That alone will make you unstoppable. Ask, wait, and receive. (Note: This can be an extremely emotional time, but it won't always be. Sometimes you may not feel as if anything happens. This is where faith comes in: we always believe we receive when we pray. If you ask, believing, you will receive according to Matthew 21:22.)

Part Four: What Now?

It's pretty easy to receive a message and file it away without ever having acted on it. I've done that too many times to count, and it has never gone well for me. To hear and not to act is to deceive ourselves. The only way to keep what you have received from God is to live it out!

20

Wimps, Whiners, and Weirdoes

One of the greatest leaders Israel has ever known was a man with a speech impediment and a radioactive face. Another hero of the faith labeled himself the biggest sissy in the entire nation. One member of the Hebrews hall of fame was a prostitute who committed treason. There's also a young man whose brothers left him in a hole and sold him as a slave. And it gets better.

The list of great believers includes a prophet who saw things so weird he could barely describe them. To this day, we read the letters of a vehement Jew who killed Christians until he was struck blind. We also highly regard a few fishermen who made a quick exit from the business, and we emulate the Christ-likeness of a guy whose final moments on earth involved getting bludgeoned to death with big rocks.

None of these people would likely get elected to a modern day hall of fame, yet God chose each of them for specific, essential tasks. Every one of them is famous in heaven.

When God called Moses, he tried to excuse himself because he had a speech impediment. Though he was one of the most courageous and humble leaders who has ever walked the earth, Moses believed his handicap would keep God's glory at bay.

Still, God chose Moses to lead Israel out of captivity and into the Promised Land. I'm positive Moses did not stutter as he faced down Pharaoh and said, "Let God's people go!"

God had to find Gideon hiding in a winepress. Gideon questioned whether God was truly with His people and claimed to be the weakest person in all of Israel. Under the power and direction of God, however, Gideon and a pitifully small collection of faithful soldiers thrashed a vicious Midianite army.

Rahab, a prostitute and a sinner under the Law, saw an opportunity for redemption when the Lord's soldiers came to her. Rather than cling to a false loyalty to a city that likely despised her, she found grace in the eyes of a Father who accepted and delivered her.

Joseph discovered the depths of misery in Egypt's prisons. The wisdom and favor of the Most High not only rescued this poor, abandoned kid, but turned him into a savior of the nation and of his people.

Can you imagine what it would have been like to have a conversation with the prophet Ezekiel? Ezekiel saw things in the Spirit that technology did not catch up with for centuries. He had a hard time describing what God showed him because he probably did not have a frame of reference for the glory he encountered. He had to make comparisons that fell far short of what he actually saw. And if you lived during that time and listened to him talk, you'd probably think he was the strangest person you ever met.

Paul, who used to be murderous Saul of Tarsus, considered himself the least of those like him. Peter, Andrew, James, and John would have been called fools for leaving behind their livelihood to follow a wandering teacher. These apostles became the foundation of the church and witnessed the awesome power of Holy Spirit even as they learned to know Him.

Stephen suffered a bone-crushing death, yet in his last moment, He saw Jesus standing at God's throne with his own human eyes!

This small sampling of the awesome men and women of God shows just a little of how God thinks. Notice that none of them considered themselves mighty or strong. Consider that not one of them had a degree from an accredited university. We would probably lock a couple of them away if they lived today.

But every one of them became great for the same reason: God was with them.

God loves the wimps, the whiners, and the weirdoes because they prove the greatness of His glory. If He chose the strong, the beautiful, and the self-righteous, humans would inevitably argue that we are powerful in ourselves. We wouldn't need God's help because our own ingenuity and strength would help us overcome. If we only studied enough, we could arrive at any revelation we needed. God would be obsolete.

So, to show us just how foolish it is to think that way, God uses the very things humans despise or belittle to put His power on display.

Qualifications in themselves are not bad, but being unqualified should not stop believers from ministering the gifts with which God has entrusted them. If someone were to defer ministry until they had achieved the necessary qualifications according to the world, they would inevitably miss out on opportunities along the way. In the kingdom, Jesus has already qualified believers. What more could we need?

Likewise, human strength is at best a risky gamble. Strengthening our bodies or minds may indeed produce good fruit, but not a single devil has left because someone physically or mentally overpowered it. I would love to punch cancer in the face, but it's just not possible.

To God's way of thinking, however, walking with the Spirit of Might should make even the weakest believer bold enough to move mountains. Greatness for believers comes from lining up with the promises of God and surrendering to Him. In my own right, I will never be great, never be qualified to live out the dreams I have, and never be powerful enough to change the world. With God, I have everything I need to do those things right now.

Put in the simplest possible terms, greatness in the kingdom comes down to hearing God and doing what He says.

Moses, Joshua, David, Daniel, Ruth, Esther, Mary, and Jesus Himself all had one thing in common: when God called them, they answered, "Yes." They gave themselves into the hands of God Almighty, and He transformed them into the heroes through which He would reach the world.

He has not changed His mode of operation.

Today, God is still searching for those whose hearts will say yes to Him. Those hearts are the ones He can mold and fill. Those faithful people stand in His shadow where fear and doubt dare not tread. Those inspired saints understand what God has tried to communicate since the beginning: He is with us. Always.

As I said in the introduction, God doesn't believe in average, un-capable Christians. He knows what gifts He has given us. He can see the final result of every command and calling before we take the first step. He Himself accompanies us to see that we cannot fail. And with God, even the most ordinary person becomes entirely extraordinary.

All it takes is to say yes.

Say yes to the dreams He has planted in your heart. They're not crazy or unreachable. They're the plans God has for you that are for your good. They're the future He has known from the beginning, the result of His innumerable thoughts about you.

Say yes to the gifts He offers. They're available to every believer according to His grace. You already have some of them. Put them to work. And if you lack anything, ask. Jesus promised God would not be stingy.

Say yes to the callings on your life. Whether they're permanent, temporary, or just for today, don't ignore the call of your Lover. Adventure and excitement accompany the unknown. Learn to silence the insidious lies of fear, and trust Jesus. The unknown is only scary if you face it with someone you don't trust. You must believe your Lord and follow wherever He leads. Jesus knows how much cooler the view is from the places that seem hard to reach. And maybe He just wants to get you alone for a minute because that's what a lover does. Will you let fear of failure rob your next encounter with Jesus?

Say yes to intimacy with God the Father, with Holy Spirit, and with Jesus. Learn to relate to God as all of these. He has expressed Himself these ways for reasons we may not fully understand this side of heaven, but He has done so for good reasons. Richness abides in the relationship.

Say yes to love. Grow in it. Live in it. Receive it. Give it away.

Doing these things may very well make you seem crazy or weird in the eyes of the world. You may very well feel weak sometimes when you recognize the power of God or the magnitude of what He's called you to, but when you get to heaven, you won't feel out of place. You'll walk in a crowd of great witnesses who have experienced the same things.

And if you're worried that you'll mess up or that you're not perfect, you'll fit right in. None of the believers I admire most were perfect, and neither am I. Welcome to the club.

Scriptures for meditation:
Hebrews 11
Exodus 3:11-22
Exodus 6:28-7:7
Judges 6:11-14
Judges 7
Joshua 1:1-9
Romans 11:29

Make it real:

• If there are any dreams in your heart you have allowed to die, ask Holy Spirit to revive them. Pay attention to what begins to burn in your heart again. Ask for direction, counsel, and might as you pursue what He brings back to you.

• Declare that you have said "yes" to the callings and gifts of God. Each day, say yes again. God loves it when you agree with Him.

• Ask for the pouring out of Holy Spirit's anointing to accomplish the desires of your heart. He knows how, when, and where to make His plans for you reality. He will empower you to walk them out.

• Renounce any judgments or lies you have agreed with concerning your dreams. Confess life and prosperity over yourself in Jesus' name. "Father, in Jesus name I renounce the judgments I have spoken against myself and my dreams when I said _____. I destroy those words back to the beginning in Jesus name. I fall out of agreement with the lie that _____. I decree that I am blessed and prospered by Your mighty hand. Because I delight in You, You will give me the desires of my heart according to your word. Thank you, Father, in Jesus' name."

21

My Testimony

I was born on December 23, 1981, in a little town in West Texas called Rankin. I arrived about a month earlier than I was supposed to because the devil tried to kill me off. In my mother's womb, the umbilical cord had become wrapped around my throat so that I was not receiving nutrition. I was slowly suffocating and starving to death.

Yet, here I am typing, a fact which I hope ticks Satan off immensely.

I had a wonderful childhood, and I earnestly believe I have a couple of the best parents I have ever met. They loved me with all their hearts and raised me well. I thank God for giving me Mom and Dad because a great deal of the revelation of His love I have received is directly related to the love I received from them. I am blessed to be their son.

Despite the wonderful raising I had, however, I still managed to stray off into the darkness. At the age of twelve, I first discovered pornography on late night television. As I grew through my teenage years, I delved deeper and deeper into that slimy world, and I lost more and more of myself to it. Even before being saved, I knew what I was doing was wrong, and I would often beg God to forgive me. Yet, as a dog returns to its vomit, so

I returned to the very thing of which I became so ashamed.

Along with my pornography habit, I had also developed enough pride to sink a ship. I was among the brightest students in my class at school, excelling at just about everything I put my hand to. Viewing life as a competition, I strove to be the best all the time. I loved the attention I got at awards ceremonies as I made trip after trip to the podium.

At my senior awards ceremony, I even refused to sit near anyone else because I wanted to have room for the plaques and certificates I assumed I would receive. "Let the average kids enjoy each other's company," I thought to myself, "I need to sit in the aisle."

I was practically drowning in error. Though I cannot recall a time when I didn't believe in God, I viewed Him as a distant floaty thing somewhere in space. I really believed that all I had to do was join a church and show up regularly so that I could get to heaven. But I had plenty of time for that. I figured I would just join a church later, after I had lived a little. Maybe when I got married and had kids I would go serve my time in the penitentiary of pews, but certainly not right now, when there was so much living to do.

Besides, I also believed I would suffer some severe punishment for my porn habit before I could be saved. I imagined some kind of "purification ceremony" I would endure at the hands of a church that would make me acceptable to God.

Also, I was far too busy getting ready for football, basketball, tennis, or whatever sport was next to be at church. To top it all off, I was fairly certain that church was incredibly boring and pointless. After all, I was a good person in my own judgment, despite the obvious sin I had, so I didn't believe I was in any danger.

In September of 1999, my outlook on life changed drastically. In the second football game of the season, I suffered a blindside hit from one of the other team's larger players. I flew backwards, fortunate not have broken my neck from the impact. When my body hit the ground, however, my left arm twisted at a strange angle under my torso. My left humerus snapped in two.

The physical trauma damaged me quite enough, but the emotional torment I soon endured overshadowed even the pain of the injury. I had lost what mattered most to me. I knew the severity of the break would keep me out of my football uniform until deep in the playoffs at the earliest. As it turned out, I never got on the field again.

At home, I couldn't sleep in my bed because the bones moved when I lay horizontally, so I slept in a recliner in the living room. I had to wear workout style pants to school because I could not zip and button jeans. I also had to wear my dad's shirts over my whole arm and sling because I could not place my arm into a sleeve. I looked ridiculous.

Outwardly, I tried to maintain a happy façade, but self-pity gnawed at my heart like a colony of termites. Pitiful as it sounds, I kept a Walkman on the end table next to my recliner so after everyone else had gone to bed, I could listen to sappy music and cry myself to sleep. When I wasn't in the mood to cry, I fantasized about murdering the player who blindsided me and sent me into this pit of misery.

That was one of the lowest times in my life. Yet, that's where Jesus found me.

A schoolmate invited me to youth group one evening, and I figured I had nothing better to do. The video we watched that night examined some bands I listened to at the time and showed that their lyrics and their messages did not honor God. Intrigued, I decided to attend church the following Sunday.

I assume other people were at the service that morning, but I could not swear to it. I felt as if the pastor and I were having a private conversation. Amazingly enough, many of the things I had misunderstood were the very things he preached about. Jesus alone could atone for my sin. He took my punishment. I would be accepted by Him if I only came. God was a Father, not a floaty thing. He wanted me.

At the evening service, on November 14, 1999, I gave my life to Jesus. It was the best thing I have ever done.

I threw myself into my new faith, devouring Bible passages like a starving man and showing up to church any time the doors opened. I learned about Jesus, about God's love, about living a moral and upright life. I felt alive again.

But I still hadn't dealt with the darker forces that had been draining the life out of me without my ever knowing it. About two months after my conversion, those forces surfaced again.

I found myself in the battle between my flesh, which seemed to have an insatiable demand for lust and pornography, and my spirit, which urged me onward toward Jesus. A cycle emerged in which I would sin willingly, wrack myself with guilt, and wallow in shame. When I decided I was sorry enough, I would seek the thrill of forgiveness, followed by a brief high before the plummet through the cycle began again.

My arrogance resurfaced as I observed my fellow churchgoers. "God," I asked one day, "how could people be this complacent about You?" When you ask a judgmental question, you get to live out the answer.

As I graduated High School and went to college, my faith became more religious exercise and intellectual pursuit than relationship. I went to church because I felt obligated to do so. I read my Bible, prayed regularly, and went about my business. By the time I graduated college, my pornography habit had more hold on my heart than did the love of Jesus.

When I got my first job teaching high school English in Sterling City, Texas, God began to draw me back to Himself. In Sterling City, I met some Christians who were truly seeking Jesus and madly in love with Him. Quite frankly, they scared the daylights out of me. Yet, they also challenged me.

Among these people were Lauren and Cliff Caldwell, who have become my dear friends. They quickly became mentors to me in the faith, and God eventually used their status in my life to alter my course.

About two years after I met her, Lauren started talking to me about something called "deliverance." She gave me a book called <u>Shadow Boxing</u> by Dr. Henry Malone and told me to read it, talk to Jesus about it, and call her if I wanted to pursue deliverance any further.

Deliverance was totally foreign to me. In the churches I had attended previously, the accepted view was basically a demons-are-scary-so-let's-not-talk-about-them approach. As I read Shadow Boxing, I could identify the open doors by which the devil had gained access to my life. I could point to fruits produced by all of the root spirits Dr. Malone outlined. I began to journal areas of my life where I could see the enemy at work. Best of all, I felt as if I could actually do something about it!

I soon called Lauren up and went through an all-night deliverance session with the Caldwells. I received incredible freedom from the Lord over most of the areas we had identified. Once again, I felt the flame of passion for Jesus burning in my heart.

But I hadn't yet decided to step all the way into the kingdom. I was still in love with my habit, so I kept it. The cycle of spiritual highs followed by shame and guilt still held me in its sway. Now, though, I dived deeper than I ever had.

I thought once I was delivered, the process should be complete. I believed I shouldn't need help again to deal with spiritual issues, so when my addiction to pornography resurfaced, I ran away from God.

I practically hid from anyone I knew with any spiritual discernment for about a year and a half. I was terrified that someone would get a word about my shameful cycle and cry me out. I felt deep in my heart that, sooner or later, I would be humiliated and rejected. Praise God He didn't abandon me in that time. He was still teaching me and calling me, but I sank to the lowest point I have ever reached.

I hated myself because I felt I had missed my opportunity to be free. I knew Jesus loved me, yet I rejected myself from His love. I felt I didn't deserve it. My self-hatred finally resulted in physical self-torture. I didn't like me, so I hurt me.

Finally, I became so desperate I reestablished contact with the Caldwells. They started feeding me truth, showing me how

Jesus had never rejected me. Danetta Ferguson, who worked at the school system where I taught, also became a trusted counselor to me during this time. I became proficient at making up reasons to visit her office, and I did so frequently.

As time passed, Holy Spirit began leading me gently and steadfastly toward total surrender to Jesus. The Lord gave me dreams that warned, corrected, and encouraged me. He had led me to people who genuinely cared about me and who did not reject me because of my past. And soon, through Danetta and the Caldwells, I met Brandy Helton.

I had heard a lot about Brandy. She was discipling Danetta and the Caldwells, so a great deal of her teaching had trickled down to me through them. From the day I met her, she began to speak over me that God had a destiny for me that was greater than I had imagined. (Brandy believes that about every single person.)

God called Brandy to found The Garden Supernatural Training Center for the purpose of equipping believers in the love of Jesus and in the weapons of spiritual warfare. From the time I heard of it, I felt the Lord drawing me there.

At first, though I was invited to play drums on the Garden's worship team, I let fear stop me from joining. Another year passed, and though Holy Spirit led me in many great strides, I was still struggling with rejection, shame, and yes, pornography.

That changed one night when God sent me a warning dream. For the sake of brevity, suffice it to say the dream rattled me to the core. The sum of the dream was this: Jesus was telling me to choose whether or not I would serve Him and Him alone.

After I shared my dream with the Caldwells, I found myself in the midst of an intense battle inside my heart. This was what Jesus had been leading me toward since the day He first saved me. He had to have my heart, all of it, and He wanted it free from those other masters I had served. Broken, with my face pressed to the floor, I finally said yes to Jesus.

Since that day in April of 2009, I have never been the same. Though it took several months longer, I overcame my pornography addiction by the blood of the Lamb. Though it has been painful at times, Jesus is teaching me to walk in humility. And after years of living in the shadows of rejection, I have received revelation of the unchangeable love of my Father God.

I joined the Garden's School of Ministry in September of 2009, and recently completed the second year of classes. I have been a part of street outreaches, healing services, and worship. I've seen people healed on the spot as Jesus is preached. I've witnessed prophecy break out in a room, with words of knowledge piercing hearts. I've felt the irresistible presence of God Almighty fall on meetings like a waterfall.

Most importantly, my heart burns for my dear Lord, and I experience His love daily.

The reason I've told you my story is that my story is just like every other saint in the kingdom. I was in darkness. Jesus saved me. I tried to run. He ran faster. He revealed Himself to me, loved me, and empowered me. He transformed me from an addict stagnating in self-hatred to a son walking in power. And the best is yet to come.

I know for a fact I have not arrived at my final destination. I am still here, after all. I am growing, learning, and sometimes failing. But the king lives in me, and I'm never going back to where I was! Hallelujah!

I hope you see in my testimony the importance of continuing to press in to God's love. I hope you understand that deliverance is not an event but a lifestyle, as God pulls out of us the things that don't belong and fills us with His power and love. Most of all, I hope you see one more example of God's unfailing, unstoppable love. I'm just another one of those wimps, whiners, and weirdoes whom God has transformed into an honored vessel of His glory.

And if He'll do it for me, I know He'll do it for you.

Scriptures for meditation:

2 Corinthians 7:1
2 Timothy 1:6-7
Psalm 72:12-14
Colossians 1:13-14
Matthew 7:15-23
Acts 2:1-13, 36-39
Hebrews 9:13-15

Make it real:

If you have never accepted Jesus as Savior and LORD, now is the time to do it! Everything in life comes down to the Lordship of Jesus Christ. Here are some Scriptures to help you:

• Romans 3:23, where you see that all have sinned.
• Romans 6:23, where you discover that the result of sin is death, which means separation from God and eternity in hell.
• John 3:16-17, which shows the love of Jesus and how anyone who believes in Him can be saved.
• Ephesians 2:8-10, which clearly proves that salvation comes by the grace of God through faith, not through works. It is a gift, which means it cannot be earned. That also means that you must receive it in order to have it.
• Acts 2:36-39, where Peter proclaims that God made Jesus Lord, which means "master," and Christ, which means "savior." These verses also call you to repent for your sins, be baptized as a sign of your faith in Jesus, and receive the Holy Spirit, who Jesus Himself promised He would send to those who belonged to Him.
• Romans 10:9-10, which teaches people how to receive salvation. Step one is to believe in your heart that Jesus is Who He says He is: the Son of God who died for your sins. Step two is to confess with your mouth that Jesus is Lord, which means you are surrendering your whole life to Him.

If you want to make Jesus your Lord, you can pray a prayer like this:

Father, I believe your Word, and I confess that I have sinned. I have disobeyed you and done wrong, which makes me worthy of hell. But Lord, your Word says you will forgive all my sins if I ask, so I ask you now to forgive every one of my sins in Jesus' name. Lord, I believe that Jesus is your Son. I believe that Jesus died on the cross for My sins, and that He is Lord of all. So now, I receive the gift of salvation, in Jesus' name. I confess that Jesus is my Lord. I surrender my life to Him. I ask to be filled with Holy Spirit according to Your promise, in Jesus' name. Thank you for saving me! In Jesus' name, Amen.

If you have made Jesus your Lord, I strongly encourage you to tell someone about it. You may even get them saved in the process. If you're not sure who to talk to about it, start with someone you know is already a Christian and has been praying for you. You will need someone to walk with you and train you up in your faith. Also, start talking directly to Holy Spirit. He is your teacher, and John 14:26 says He will teach you all things.

22

Go, Therefore

Jesus' final command as recorded in the gospel of Matthew was for His followers to go and make disciples of all the world. But He didn't just tell them to leave, He said, "Go, therefore..." What is it that Jesus deemed our biggest reason to go?

Matthew 28:18 says, "All authority has been given to Me in heaven and on earth." In heaven and on earth, Jesus has it all, which leaves none for the enemy. Perhaps that is why He instructed us to pray that God's will be done on earth just as in heaven.

Jesus has the right to make it so.

And Jesus, the rightful holder of all authority, restored God's original mandate for man to spread His dominion over all the earth. He manifests Himself to those who love Him. He destroys the work of the devil. He delivers from darkness and plants into the kingdom of light. Jesus reigns.

I found it fascinating when I learned that at the beginning the church didn't call itself "the church." The body of Christ called itself "the Way." Soon after I learned that, Holy Spirit connected that name to John the Baptist's life message.

When John bellowed from the rooftops that people should

prepare the way of the Lord, he wasn't only talking about a physical pathway. He also referred to the hearts of those who heard. John's preaching, put in different terms, could be understood, "Prepare Jesus a throne in your heart."

The Bible shows that Jesus wasn't looking for a place to visit; He was looking for a place to dwell. His greatest desire is and always has been to be with His people. And Jesus Himself declares, "I am with you always, to the very end."

That means the primary center of Jesus' reign, His capital city in the world so to speak, is in the hearts of the believers. If Christians truly are the hands and feet of Jesus, the image of our king to this world, then we are also the way by which He invades the earth.

That by itself is enough to make anyone special. Friend, I may never have met you, but I know without a doubt that you are an extraordinary person. In your lifetime, you have accomplished amazing things, and the best is yet to come. You are unique, fashioned by the Creator and filled by the Living Breath of God. You are a masterpiece. You powerfully grace the lives of those around you just by being who you are.

You are a gateway through which the king of kings arrives on the earth and transforms it into His never ending kingdom. In your heart, Jesus, the Lamb of God and the Lion of Judah, sits enthroned in majesty. Through your words and actions, the world will know of Him.

That is the heritage Jesus gave you. You have a piece of a wonderful puzzle the world needs, and without you, the picture will never be complete. Someone out there needs you specifically to love them like Jesus. Someone needs your face to reflect His glory, your hands to bring His healing, and your presence to carry the comfort of His peace.

They're waiting right now. You must obey the Master and go.

Go to your church family and share what God has given you. Go to your relatives and love them with the love Father pours out on you. Go to the lost, the broken, and the fearful and tell them about the Great Comforter sent by Jesus Himself to lead them to Him. Go to your secret place and be with Jesus so He can fill you up with the love you need to get out the door.

Go have fun with Him.

Our beautiful king is calling all of us to higher places far beyond our comfort zones. That is where Jesus uses us to change the world. That's where we discover more and more of Who our God is, and who we are in Him.

Jesus regained all authority at the cross, and He has passed it on to us with the command that we go. When we obey, we become the way by which Jesus comes, and when Jesus comes, miracles happen.

I may never know of your exploits with Jesus this side of heaven, but I will be thrilled to meet you there and share stories of what He did in us, to us, and through us.

And as you turn this last page, may your heart burn with passion for the One Who calls you. May your prayers ignite the fire in His heart. May your courage rise within you. May your ears be sharpened to hear the call. May God Almighty anoint you with power and the Holy Spirit, and may you always and everywhere go about doing good.

That's what Jesus did, and you're just like Him.

Go, therefore, and Godspeed.

Kevin McSpadden lives in San Angelo, Texas, with his wife Karen and their dog, Zeke. The McSpaddens attend The Garden Gathering, where they continue to learn about King Jesus and His amazing kingdom. Kevin teaches English at Miles High School near San Angelo. He loves to fish, read, and play the drums with Rivers Rising, the worship team at The Garden. He is a normal Christian who loves Jesus and believes signs, miracles, and wonders happen every day.

CPSIA information can be obtained
at www.ICGtesting.com
Printed in the USA
LVHW050444230520
656338LV00006B/628